Mennonites and Their Heritage

A Handbook of Mennonite History and Beliefs

Part I. Mennonite Origins and the Mennonites of Europe
BY HAROLD S. BENDER

Part II. Mennonites in America
BY C. HENRY SMITH

WIPF & STOCK · Eugene, Oregon

Wipf and Stock Publishers
199 W 8th Ave, Suite 3
Eugene, OR 97401

Mennonites and Their Heritage
A Handbook of Mennonite History and Beliefs
By Bender, Harold S. and Smith, C. Henry
Copyright © 1976 Herald Press, All rights reserved.
Softcover ISBN-13: 978-1-7252-8326-8
Publication date 6/16/2020
Previously published by Herald Press, 1976

Foreword

MENNONITES AND THEIR HERITAGE (1942, 1944) was first published by the Mennonite Central Committee as a series of six booklets, each by a different writer. These booklets were designed primarily to serve as texts for study by men in Civilian Public Service camps.

The first two of these booklets, *Mennonite Origins in Europe*, by Harold S. Bender, and *Mennonites in America*, by C. Henry Smith, have continued to be in demand as brief and effective presentations of Mennonite history. Since both of the authors are now deceased, Guy F. Hershberger and Cornelius Krahn have brought these booklets up to date, and the Mennonite Publishing House is making them available in this combined format under the title of the original series.

Here the reader has available a brief survey of Mennonite history in Europe and America. It can serve as a text for class study, or for general reading.

The story of Mennonite origins and development is an entrancing one. It is important for understanding Mennonite doctrine and life. Knowing the history of their church is sure to give members an appreciation of their heritage; it also gives a sense of direction as the church endeavors to live its life and give its witness in today's world.

The publisher is therefore glad to make available a book which gives authentic information for individual readers, for class study, and for permanent record in libraries.   —PAUL ERB.

Contents

PART I

MENNONITE ORIGINS AND THE MENNONITES OF EUROPE

BY HAROLD S. BENDER

A. The Soil of the Mennonite Faith

CHAPTER 1

The Beginning and Growth of the Christian Church

Nineteen hundred years ago and more, One came to earth from the heavenly glory, the only begotten Son of the Father, full of grace and truth, Jesus Christ, the Saviour of the world. He humbled Himself and took upon Himself the form of a servant, and became obedient unto death, even the death of the cross. This same Jesus invited men to believe on Him, to learn of Him, and to follow Him. To as many as believed He gave the power to become the sons of God, and with these disciples and believers He established His church upon the rock, the church against which the gates of hell shall not prevail. To this church He gave a great commission, to go into all the world and preach the Gospel to every creature, and to teach them to observe all things whatsoever He commanded. This church He endowed with the power of the Holy Spirit on the day of Pentecost, A.D. 30, in the city of Jerusalem, so that they were able to preach His Gospel with power unto the saving of countless thousands of men.

We of today are the heirs of the faith and life of this church. Because these disciples of old and their successors to this day have carried the Gospel unto the uttermost parts of the earth and have built the church in every land, and have followed in the footsteps of Jesus and kept His commandments, we have entered into the kingdom of God, and have become disciples of Christ. The unbroken chain of faith down through the ages, the never-ceasing preaching of the Gospel, the devoted discipleship of Christians through the centuries, these things have brought us the Gospel which makes us joint heirs with Christ. Because of them we are Christians today. True, we have made our own choice, we have chosen to accept Christ as *our* Saviour, and to endeavor to keep His Word, but this opportunity would never have come to us had it not been for the church of the past nineteen centuries.

Most modern Mennonites are the descendants of Teutonic tribes of what is now Switzerland, Germany, and Holland, who lived in heathen darkness until the missionaries of the church found them in the early Middle Ages and brought the gospel to them. Swiss, Dutch, and German people they were, who were evangelized after a fashion by Roman Catholic missionaries in the seventh and eighth centuries, and who until the time of the Reformation in the sixteenth century continued in the faith and worship of the Roman Catholic Church.

What kind of church was this which brought our Teutonic ancestors into the fold of Christ?

The Catholic Church of the Middle Ages was the direct descendant of the early church founded at Jerusalem on the day of Pentecost in the year A.D. 30, which had through valiant missionary endeavors spread over the whole known world and gradually, by about the year A.D. 1000, brought Christianity to all of Europe. This was a great achievement. We of modern times with our missionary organization on a great scale have not yet equaled their victorious conquest of the world in which they lived. For this we honor the early church and acknowledge its faith and power.

Nevertheless, along with this great expansion and missionary conquest, along with its maintenance of the true faith and worship of God and Jesus Christ as Saviour, we find that strange and remarkable changes took place in the church which were for the most part not only undesirable, but positively evil. The simple faith and organization, the pure life and effective work of the early New Testament church, were transformed into a complex organization, partially perverted doctrines, and sadly declining life and morals. Many of the most precious possessions of faith of the early church were forfeited by these changes, and consequently in many respects the Catholic Church of the Middle Ages was no longer the true church of Christ. Let us trace some of these changes.

In the first place, the church which Christ established was composed of believers only, men and women who had personal experience of faith in Him, who knew that their sins were forgiven, and who pledged their lives to Him as their Lord in trust and obedience. During the centuries that followed it came to be the custom to include everyone in the church, primarily by the rite of baptism shortly after

10

birth. Thus the church was no longer composed of persons who had repented of their sins and been born again by the Spirit of God, but of the entire population of those countries which had accepted nominal Christianity. Many of these people were true believers, but many more were traditional Christians, simply following the customs and ways of the times. Nominally they were Christians, but actually they were without an inner heart experience of salvation and with no commitment to live a life of holiness and to keep the commandments of Christ.

In the second place, the organization of the church was transformed from that of a simple, practical form of church government, under the leadership of local ministers and elders, into a great ecclesiastical institution with centralized authority in the hands of the bishops and archbishops, culminating in one dictatorial authority, the pope. In this church the members were the subjects of the church, the ordained priests and bishops constituting the church in reality. Many of these priests and bishops were unworthy of the office and power which they held, to say nothing of the fact that such a form of church government is neither taught nor recognized in the New Testament as a right form of government for the church.

In the third place, contact with God was no longer possible except through the priests of the church. The blessings of God and His grace were available to the people solely through the ministry of the priest, and in particular through the performance of certain ceremonies known as the seven sacraments, which included baptism, the Lord's Supper, and similar ordinances. Thus, for the average Christian the Christian life meant not faith in Christ and personal experience of the grace of God, and an obedience to the teaching of Christ and the apostles as found in the New Testament, but rather obedience to the priest, receiving the ceremonies of the church, and obeying the rules of the church as made known through the priest.

In the fourth place, salvation was accordingly not secured through faith in Christ, but through performance of the works required by the church. The great doctrine of justification by faith as it is taught by the Apostle Paul in the Book of Romans and elsewhere, the forgiveness of sins through the precious sacrifice of Christ on the cross—all this was in reality lost. Instead, there was substituted a formal system of religion, with faith in the performance of church ceremonies and good works, which is much like the religion of certain of the more advanced heathen peoples. That there were large numbers of hungry hearts, who not having found the Gospel did not find peace with God, and who were seeking a better way than that which they had, goes without saying. The restless seeking after the true life hid with Christ in God was expressed in a great multiplication of religious forms and outward worship which did not satisfy. Lacking inner peace and seeking something better, large numbers of Christians, both men and women, decided to follow the advice given by the church and enter monasteries and convents which were established in great number in the Middle Ages. There, by sacrificing the ordinary way of life, by giving up the privilege of marriage and family life, private property, private independence and freedom, and by the performance of good works, they sought the peace which they were unable to find elsewhere.

In the fifth and last place, since the mass of Christians never had the privilege of reading the New Testament firsthand, and were required to worship in a service conducted in the Latin language which they could not understand, and since they seldom heard the preaching of the Gospel or the admonition to holiness and righteous living which only those who preach the Word of God in its purity can give, standards of morals sank lower and lower. Great masses of Christians paid no attention at all to the ideals for living which Christians today consider necessary, not because they desired to be evil, but because they did not know how to be otherwise. Through the centuries ways of living grew up which were far from Christian. A few wealthy landholders oppressed the peasants into serfdom so that they were practically slaves to their masters. There was much injustice, oppression, and abuse. Immorality was widespread, and brutality and violence were practiced on every hand. Many priests and bishops of the church lived on a low level of morals, in some respects being even worse than the common people in the practice of the prevailing sins of the age.

In the light of these serious and dreadful changes and perversions which took place in the professing church through the centuries, it is almost a marvel that the true faith survived at all. That it did survive is due chiefly to two things. In the first place, in spite of the fact that the Holy Scriptures were not made available to the people, and were read chiefly in Latin by the priests of the church during the Middle Ages, the Scriptures were preserved. They were there for anyone to find in them the truth of the Gospel, and to bring revival. In the second place, there were faithful and devoted followers of

Christ in all the centuries, even though their number may have been small, very small at times. Here and there were individuals who endeavored in spite of the corruption and decay of the church to live lives of holiness and purity. Here and there were small organized groups who endeavored to revive and reform the church. Sometimes revivals broke out, as a result of which thousands of Christians were led to better things. Again and again, however, the official church persecuted these groups, sometimes with a brutality and a severity which brought martyrdom to thousands. Very little is known of some of these earnest Christians through the centuries, although the names of some of the groups and a few of their leaders have been handed down to us.

The most important of these groups were two, the Waldenses, founded by Peter Waldo of Lyons, France, about 1170, and the Brethren of the Common Life, who existed in Holland and Western Germany from the fourteenth century on. After the year 1300 stronger movements for reform arose, led by great and influential leaders such as John Wycliffe (1324-84) in England, and John Huss (1370-1415) in Bohemia. Persecution, however, destroyed every attempt to reform the church in a larger way.

In the midst of this darkness, God in His mercy and power brought a great revival to pass. This revival, commonly known as the Protestant Reformation, is the most important thing that has happened in the history of the church since the apostolic days.

CHAPTER 2

The Reformation and Its Fruits

The great revival which came to the church in the sixteenth century, known as the Protestant Reformation, is of particular interest to Mennonites, because it was out of this revival movement that the Mennonite Church was born. We must therefore seek to understand what was happening in Switzerland, Germany, and Holland in the Reformation so that we may know how our own church came into existence.

In the providence of God, a leader arose in the church in Germany in the early years of the sixteenth century who had a vision of what the Christian experience of salvation ought to be in the light of the teachings of Christ and the apostles in the New Testament. Because he found in his own experience that it was alone through faith in the atoning work of Christ that the sinner could find forgiveness for his sins and have peace with God, and because he felt that this great experience of justification through faith alone was the very heart of the Gospel, this man was irresistibly impelled to testify to this great truth and to proclaim it to men everywhere. This leader was Martin Luther (1483-1546), who lived most of his life in the town of Wittenberg in Saxony, about seventy miles southwest of what is now Berlin, Germany.

In addition to a deep devotion to the great truth of the Gospel which he had found in his own experience, Martin Luther also had a strong conviction that the Word of God alone should be the source of all Christian truth, and that only through this way could men come to faith and life in the Gospel.

Not only did Martin Luther believe these great fundamental truths of justification by faith alone, and the exclusive authority of the Word of God, but he also had great character and power of will. Once he found the truth of God, he was determined to give his life to it, regardless of what might happen. It was as a young professor

14

in the University of Wittenberg that he first began to teach and to preach the great truths on which the Reformation was founded. An able preacher and writer, he soon found a remarkable response in his students, among the Christians of his town, throughout all Germany, and in fact throughout all Europe. Everywhere men had been hungry for the Gospel which he had rediscovered. Everywhere they were eager to find the way to God through faith in Christ, and to discard the degraded and corrupt Roman Catholic Church with its salvation by works, its denial of the Bible to the people, and its dreadful burden of ceremony and forms imposed by the priests.

So it was that within a very few years after Martin Luther's first proclamation of the new discovery in 1517, thousands of Christians in all parts of Europe flocked to his banner. Luther had at first not intended to found a new church, but rather to reform the old church. Soon he saw, however, that the authorities of the Roman Catholic Church were determined to crush him and the movement which had gathered around his preaching, and by the year 1525 he concluded that there was no other way but to organize a new church which would do away with Catholic practices, doctrines, and organization, and pattern its faith, life, and organization after the New Testament. So he set up what has since been known as the Lutheran Church, or the Evangelical Church of Germany. In a few short years this church spread throughout most of northern and central Germany, and all of Denmark, Norway, Sweden, and Finland, as well as other scattered places in Europe. In fact, the Lutheran movement was so powerful that it seemed about to sweep all of Europe and to overthrow completely the Roman Catholic Church.

Martin Luther, however, failed in his original intention of establishing a pure Christian church based upon the New Testament only. He was too much bound in his thinking to the traditions and customs of the past, and was unwilling to go the whole way in breaking away from Catholic practices. He originally intended to establish a church composed of believers only, but when he saw the low state of spirituality and morals among the masses of the people, he feared that by so doing most of the people would be outside of the evangelical church, and would thus be left to the Catholic Church. Accordingly, he made up his mind that the best plan would be to take over the entire population into his new church, and seek to use the spiritual-minded members and leaders of the church to lead the unspiritual and carnal members into a deeper experience. Thus, the Lutheran Church

15

was established as a universal state church, with infant baptism required of all and with no serious attempt to exclude from the church those who were guilty of sin and failure. This idea of a universal state church Luther took over from the Catholic Church, but he did not take over the Catholic system of church government through bishops, archbishops, and pope.

The compromise which Luther made was a very serious one. Because of this compromise it became impossible to establish a truly evangelical New Testament church according to the teachings of Christ and the apostles. There was no true discipline in the church. Many Christians continued to be guilty of unchristian living in the Lutheran Church just as they had been before in the Catholic Church. In fact, many misunderstood Luther's doctrine of spiritual liberty and salvation by faith, and assumed that as long as they professed the proper doctrines, they would not need to pay much attention to the life. Morals in many Lutheran districts at first sank lower than they had been in the Catholic Church. Thus we see that there was both great good, and some evil, in the Lutheran movement. A long step forward had been taken through the re-establishment of the doctrine of justification by faith, but much still remained to be done. We owe a great debt to Martin Luther, but we must never forget that our forefathers, as Mennonites, were unwilling to accept the Lutheran church system and for that reason were persecuted by the Lutherans in their time.

The most serious charge which must be brought against Luther and his movement is that he agreed to the principle of permitting the ruler of a territory to determine the religion of the people of that territory, and that he further agreed, indeed advocated, that force should be used to persecute those who refused to accept the religion authorized by the ruler. This principle remained in force, even in Protestant countries, for two hundred years or more after the Reformation, and led to severe persecution and death for thousands of people, particularly our own Mennonite forefathers.

As the Reformation spread throughout Europe, other leaders arose in addition to Martin Luther who were more uncompromising in their break with Catholicism. These leaders in a general way may be grouped together in one group as Calvinists or Reformed. Since the first Anabaptists or Mennonites arose in Switzerland where the Reformed type of Protestantism was dominant, we should become better acquainted with this movement.

The first leader of this group was Ulrich Zwingli (1484-1531), a Protestant preacher in Zurich, Switzerland, from 1519 to 1531. Both Zwingli and his followers in general accepted the doctrines and policies of the Lutherans. But they differed on one fundamental point. This point was, that the ordinances of baptism and the Lord's Supper had only symbolic meaning and no value in themselves as vehicles of God's grace and blessing. However, this difference was sufficiently great to keep the Zwinglians and the Lutherans apart. In addition, the Zwinglians were inclined to be more strict in their demands for righteous living by Christians, and emphasized more the doctrine of obedience to God than the inward experience of forgiveness of sin. Thus on the whole the Reformed movement was more aggressive in attempting to apply Christian principles to life. However, they made the same compromise as the Lutherans in establishing state churches inclusive of the entire population of the country. Zwingli began his preaching of the Reformation in Zurich in 1519 and from his pulpit in this city exercised great influence over the Swiss Reformation until his death in 1531. Most of the population of Switzerland north of the Alps followed his leadership into the Protestant camp, as was also the case in certain sections of southwestern Germany.

Shortly after Zwingli's death another great leader arose who became the dominant figure among the Reformed branch of the Protestant movement, even though he was a Frenchman and exerted his influence chiefly from his post as leader of the Protestant church in Geneva, Switzerland. This man was John Calvin (1509-64).

Calvin was one of the greatest leaders of the Christian Church, and next to Martin Luther the most influential figure in the history of the Protestant Reformation. A man of unusual ability as a writer and speaker, of deep conviction and determined to lead the church into full obedience to the will of God, Calvin threw himself with all his rich gifts of mind and character into the battle to establish a thoroughgoing Protestant church. Through his influence it seemed for a time that all of France would become Protestant, but unfortunately the power of the Catholics was too great, and ultimately the Catholics were able by force of arms to suppress and destroy most of the French Protestant movement. A small remnant remains, often called "Huguenots."

Meanwhile Calvin's influence through his writings reached farther and farther, especially through his great doctrinal book, published in 1536, called *Institutes of the Christian Religion*. Refugees from England and Scotland found their way to him at Geneva and returned home again to plant the influence of John Calvin's teaching firmly in England and Scotland. One of these refugees, John Knox (1515-72), became the leader of the Scottish Reformation, and established Calvinism as a form of Protestantism in that country. He exerted his greatest influence as a preacher in Edinburgh from 1559 to 1572. Since both Calvin and Knox taught a form of church government which included the use of a body of elders or presbyters as a governing body in each church, the Scottish reformed church came to be known in time as the Presbyterian Church, although its official name remained "The Church of Scotland." In England, although the Reformation was greatly influenced by Calvin's teaching and its doctrine was largely Calvinistic in character, the church itself never became Presbyterian.

Calvinism also became the dominant faith in Holland after 1560, where the Reformed Church became the established church.

The Reformation had a stormy time in England, but after a long period of ups and downs from 1531 to 1580, it finally won England fully under Queen Elizabeth I. The Church of England became largely Calvinistic in doctrine but episcopal in government.

The Protestant Reformation made great strides within the first generation after Luther began his work. However, the Roman Catholic Church was not dead. It rallied all its forces in a tremendous struggle to drive out Protestantism, crush the Protestant churches, and bring back the lost territory to the fold of the mother church. Thus began a great conflict which lasted over a hundred years, 1521-1648. During the latter part of this struggle the Catholic countries of Europe engaged in a great war of extermination against the Protestant countries. This war, lasting from 1618 to 1648, has been known as the Thirty Years' War. In the end neither side won, both sides agreeing in 1648 to mutual toleration. Thus finally after almost a century and a half the religious situation in Europe was stabilized. Most of northern Europe, including the Scandinavian countries, two thirds of Germany, most of Switzerland, all of Holland, and all of England and Scotland, with scattered sections in France and Hungary, had become Protestant. The remainder of Europe, including France, Spain and Portugal, Italy, Austria, Bohemia, and Poland, remained Catholic. Eastern Europe, including Russia and the Balkan countries, being in the fold of the Greek Orthodox Church, was not at all influenced by the

Protestant Reformation. This part of Europe seemed to be in another world.

The Reformation had great and blessed results for the progress of the Church of Christ. It freed half of Europe from its deadening bondage to Roman Catholicism and opened the way for millions of Christians to read the Bible for themselves, to have a personal, warm, and living Christian experience, and to proclaim the Gospel of free salvation by faith in Christ to the entire world. Gradually the bondage of superstition and fear, and of an outward formal religion, was cast off, and a new and more progressive and vital type of Christianity was established. Had it not been for the establishment of state churches with their intolerance and persecution of those who did not accept the creed of the state church, still more rapid progress would have been possible. Even so the Protestant countries of Europe, particularly England, Germany, Holland, and Switzerland, have been leaders in the forefront of progress, both materially and spiritually, ever since that time.

But with all its blessings, it must be remembered that the Reformation was not a satisfactory restoration of Christianity to its true, original character as intended by Christ. Its great weakness was the failure to insist upon a transformation of life and society into a truly Christian way of life in full obedience to Christ's teachings. This failure the Anabaptist-Mennonite movement proposed to make good.

B. The First Mennonites and Their Faith

CHAPTER 3

The Beginning of the Swiss Mennonites

The Mennonite faith had its origin in Switzerland in Reformation times. Certain followers of Ulrich Zwingli were unable to accept the compromise which he and Luther made in setting up a Protestant state church system. They and many others like them in western Europe had been expecting a complete reformation of the church, and a restoration of the New Testament Christianity taught by Jesus and the apostles. They wanted the church to be composed of believers only, men and women who had an experience with God and who had committed their lives in unreserved obedience to His Word. They wanted no half-Christian profession following the customs and traditions of the time, and maintaining an outward form of godliness but denying the power thereof. It was these people who completed the Reformation which Luther and Zwingli began. They were the founders of the Mennonite fellowship.

It must be kept in mind of course that the founders of the Mennonite brotherhood in Switzerland did not adopt the name "Mennonite" for the new fellowship which they established. This name was given to it much later. In fact, even today the Mennonites of Switzerland do not have it as their official name. The name "Mennonite" was given to that branch of the church which was established in Holland, in which Menno Simons became the leader after the year 1536. It was only later that the name "Mennonite" was carried over from Holland into Germany and into Switzerland, and finally into America. The first name of the church in Switzerland was simply "Brethren." These Brethren had no other name. Since there were Brethren in various places in Europe in the course

20

of the following years, it soon became the custom to refer to the ones who first founded the church in Switzerland as the Swiss Brethren. The enemies of the Brethren called them "Anabaptists" because the Brethren refused to accept infant baptism as a valid baptism and insisted upon adults being baptized upon confession of their faith. The name "Anabaptist" means literally "rebaptizer." Thus, in history, the early Mennonites in Switzerland, as well as elsewhere in Europe, are formally known by the name "Anabaptist." This is rather confusing, since other groups, somewhat similar to the Mennonites, particularly in the matter of insisting upon adult baptism, were also called Anabaptists, and thus the name came to be used to refer to a number of religious groups, some of which had radically different viewpoints on certain questions from the Mennonites proper.

The birthplace of the Mennonite Church is to be found in the city of Zurich, Switzerland, in the year 1525. The City Council of Zurich had decided to suppress the small company of people in Zurich under the leadership of Conrad Grebel, Felix Manz, and George Blaurock, who had refused to have their children baptized and who insisted that a thoroughgoing reformation should take place in accordance with Zwingli's original promise. Before taking radical measures, however, the City Council had decided to give the Brethren a chance to defend themselves in public in a debate in which Zwingli and his friends were to refute the arguments against infant baptism. As soon as the debate was over, the City Council issued strict decrees forbidding them to meet, to teach, and to have fellowship together. The little group of devoted Brethren who felt in their hearts deeply convinced that they should follow the teachings of the New Testament completely, and who endeavored to set up a church according to the pattern of Christ and the apostles, were faced with tragic alternatives. If they surrendered their position, they would be untrue to their conscience, but if they refused to obey the edict of the Council, they would be subject to persecution and arrest. In their extremity they met together for prayer, seeking guidance from God, the date being about January 21, 1525. They found the guidance they sought and were convinced that they should institute a brotherhood of believers upon the basis of baptism and confession of faith. In that meeting they baptized one another, Conrad Grebel baptizing George Blaurock, and Blaurock baptizing the remainder of the group. From that

21

meeting they went forth with joyful conviction that they should continue their fellowship, and should teach and preach their faith, and summon men everywhere to become members of the body of Christ. Thus the Mennonite Church was founded in a prayer meeting.

The story of this meeting, which is contained in an eyewitness account in the Hutterian Chronicle, is so moving that it is well worth publishing here.

Conrad Grebel, Felix Manz, and others came together and found that there was among themselves agreement in faith. They realized in the sincere fear of God that it was firstly necessary to obtain from the divine Word and the preaching of the same a true faith which worketh by love, and then to receive the true Christian baptism upon the confessed faith, as the answer of a good conscience toward God (1 Peter 3:21), being resolved henceforth to serve God in all godliness of a holy Christian life and to be steadfast in affliction (persecution) to the end.

And it further came to pass, as they were assembled together, that great anxiety came upon them and they were moved in their hearts. Then they unitedly bowed their knees before God Almighty in heaven and called upon Him, the Searcher of all hearts, and implored Him to grant them grace to do His divine will, and that He would bestow upon them His mercy. For flesh and blood and human forwardness did by no means lead them to take such a step, for they knew what would fall to their lot to suffer and endure on account of it.

After they had risen from their prayer, George Blaurock arose and earnestly asked Conrad Grebel to baptize him with the true Christian baptism upon his faith and knowledge. And entreating him thus, he knelt down and Conrad baptized him, since there was at this time no ordained minister to administer this ordinance. After this was done, the others likewise asked George to baptize them. He fulfilled their desire in the sincere fear of God, and thus they gave themselves unitedly to the name of the Lord. Then some of them were chosen for the ministry of the Gospel, and they began to teach and keep the faith.

Conrad Grebel (1498-1526), son of a wealthy iron merchant and a leading citizen of the city of Zurich and indeed of all Switzerland, was the leader of the group. He was still a young man, not more than twenty-five years of age, endowed with great gifts and well trained in six years of university study at Basel, Vienna, and Paris. The remainder of the group were largely average citizens of the city of Zurich, a baker, a tailor, a cooper, a bookseller, a goldsmith, and others of the middle classes. But it made no difference what their occupation or what their class was. They were all possessed of a great vision, and a deep and confident faith in God, and dedicated their lives unreservedly to the practice and the preaching of their faith.

During the following months and years, the witness and life of the Brethren and their aggressive missionary endeavors led to a rapid and far-reaching spread of the new church. The Swiss government authorities of Zurich and neighboring cantons tried every means to stop the movement short of the death penalty, but they failed. Imprisonment, exile, torture, fine, all were of no avail. Finally, in January, 1527, they imposed the death penalty, the first of the martyrs in Zurich being Felix Manz. Conrad Grebel had died a few months before of the plague. George Blaurock was burned at the stake two years later in Tyrol, after his exile from Zurich. But still the movement grew, and for almost a hundred years there was a strong and vigorous church in the country round about Zurich. The last martyr of this district was Hans Landis, who was executed in the year 1614. As late as 1750 there were still a few scattered remnants of the church in the Canton of Zurich.

Meanwhile the movement became even more vigorous in neighboring Swiss cantons such as Berne and Basel, and in neighboring districts of Austria, Tyrol, and South Germany. Wherever the Brethren went they founded churches, and wherever the churches were founded the authorities desperately tried to stamp out the movement by persecution and execution. For almost three hundred years this persecution continued in Switzerland, but, praise God, the authorities were not able to destroy the church, and there are still fourteen churches in Switzerland with a membership of about 1,900 baptized persons. The oldest church is that in Langnau in the Emmenthal, which has existed since 1528. We shall learn more of the experiences of these Swiss Mennonites in a later chapter.

However, the bitter persecution did succeed in destroying the church in all the neighboring territories of South Germany, Austria, and Tyrol. It is true that one branch of the church in Austria, which in 1528 under the leadership of Jacob Hutter and others had adopted Christian communism as a way of life, and were accordingly called Hutterian Brethren, were able to maintain themselves for a long time in their native land. But they also were finally driven out and by about the year 1770 the last remnant of this group had been forced to flee to Russia, from whence they all migrated to South Dakota in the years 1874-80. In 1963 the Hutterites, with a total baptized membership of nearly 14,000, were living in nearly 120 settlements, known as "Bruderhofs," in Alberta, Saskatchewan, Manitoba, Ontario, South Dakota, North Dakota, Montana, and Washington. The story of this group will be told in a later chapter.

Meanwhile the message of the Brethren had traveled far and wide by leaps and bounds. Through traveling missionaries it finally found lodging in the extreme northwest part of Germany in the city of Emden in 1530, and from there traveled over into Holland to the city of Amsterdam in the same year, and shortly after to other regions in the Netherlands. From this seed came the founding of the Mennonite church in Holland, as will be related in a later chapter.

Enemies of the Swiss Brethren did their best to destroy the movement in its very beginning by misrepresentation and abuse as well as by persecution. They were falsely accused of all sorts of crimes and wickedness by men like Zwingli, who became desperate in their opposition as they discovered the spiritual power of the new church and the appeal it made to the masses. A common charge was that the Brethren were a revolutionary and seditious party aiming at the overthrow of the state and society. Such accusations remind one of the charge against Paul that he was "turning the world upside down." It is needless to say that these charges were untrue and have been so proved by historians, but it is no wonder that the enemies of our forefathers thought they were "revolutionary" in view of the demand they made that all of life should be made fully Christian. Such action will always seem revolutionary to a world which has been lulled into a false sense of security by a compromising, easygoing half-Christianity.

CHAPTER 4

Early Swiss Mennonite Leaders

The Mennonite Church was blessed with able and courageous leaders in its early years, who were truly men of God. The achievements of these men are the more remarkable when we consider the tremendous obstacles under which they had to labor. Men like Martin Luther, Ulrich Zwingli, John Calvin, and John Knox, even though they at times had to labor under great difficulty, and frequently had to exercise courage and faith, nevertheless had an easy road compared to the founders of the Mennonite Church. When Martin Luther was in danger he found protection from the king of his country, and throughout his labors as a reformer he found rulers of states and armies placed at the disposal of the evangelical cause to defend it against its Catholic enemies and to promote its expansion. Never did Martin Luther have to suffer persecution, and seldom was the Lutheran Church suppressed in its own territory. Ulrich Zwingli was the recognized leader of his own canton, fully supported by the government of his state, and authorized to be the leader of an army in defense of Swiss Protestantism. John Calvin was a dominant figure in the government of the city of Geneva for a generation, and John Knox was the officially appointed and salaried pastor of a great city church. By contrast, most of the early leaders of the Mennonite Church died as martyrs, while their followers were hounded, persecuted, and executed. In spite of this, men of unusual ability and character gladly took upon themselves the leadership of the "accursed sect of the Anabaptists" and gave their lives "for the brethren." We have space to consider but a few of these great men—Conrad Grebel, Felix Manz, George Blaurock, Michael Sattler, and Pilgram Marpeck.

25

Conrad Grebel, c.1498-1526

Conrad Grebel may truly be called the founder of the Mennonite Church. Had it not been for his faith and devotion, and his courageous assumption of the leadership of the first group of Brethren, there might never have been a Mennonite Church. Born in Zurich, Switzerland, about 1498, of a rich and influential titled family, Conrad came from the highest social class of Switzerland. His father was an outstanding member of the City Council of Zurich, a wealthy iron merchant, who served repeatedly as ambassador of the Canton of Zurich to the meetings of the Swiss Confederacy.

The son of such a family would naturally have the advantage of the best that the world of his time could give him. He mingled with the best families of Switzerland (his sister married the noted Dr. von Watt, burgomaster of St. Gall, and formerly rector of the University of Vienna), enjoyed all the privileges which wealth could buy, and was marked for an outstanding career in his native land. Receiving a grant from the King of Austria, he studied for three years (1515-18) at the University of Vienna, after having earlier spent one year at the University of Basel. Following this he spent two years at the University of Paris with a scholarship from the King of France. Altogether he spent six years in the best universities of his time, receiving a thorough training in humanistic studies and becoming a master of Latin and Greek. As a talented scholar he looked forward to an attractive career in his native land.

How Grebel came to be the leader of a "despised sect" is a thrilling story. He was not deeply religious in his university days. In fact, on the contrary he lived the typical life of a carefree and loose-living university student. On his return to his home in 1520, he came under the influence of the brilliant and powerful new evangelical preacher in Zurich, Ulrich Zwingli, who had assumed the pulpit in January, 1519. Zwingli, himself an able scholar, gathered around him the young men of Zurich and inspired them with the challenge of the Gospel. Like many others, Conrad Grebel was thoroughly converted and threw himself enthusiastically into the great work of reforming the church. He became Zwingli's most ardent supporter and was soon known, even beyond the confines of his own city, as one of the promising future evangelical leaders.

However, Grebel soon found himself in conflict with Zwingli, the man who had won him for the Gospel. Being a devoted and able student of the New Testament in the original Greek, he became convinced that only a complete and thoroughgoing reform of the church after the pattern of the New Testament would be sufficient. To his dismay, however, he discovered that Ulrich Zwingli was not ready for such a thoroughgoing reform, but preferred to make a compromise with the existing traditions and establish a state church. When Grebel, learning this, demanded of Zwingli that he proceed with the establishment of a church of believers only, with true Gospel discipline and with a program of a thoroughgoing application of Christianity and the teachings of Jesus to everyday life, Zwingli refused.

The break with Zwingli came in 1524. Those who shared Grebel's views met with him for Bible study and prayer and rallied to the standard of a full Gospel reform. Condemned by Zwingli in the bitterest terms, Grebel sought contacts with other leaders with whom he could associate; however, all these attempts failed and when the City Council of Zurich finally condemned Grebel's entire group and forbade him and his friends to teach and preach their faith, the die was cast.

Grebel's career was a short one. Out of the eighteen months from the founding of the church in January, 1525, until his death of the plague in the summer of 1526, at least nine months were spent in prison. The remainder of the time he spent largely in itinerant evangelism in the neighboring cantons of Switzerland. He hoped to write an exposition of his faith, in defense of the principles of the church, but was prevented from doing so, except for one small pamphlet written in prison, which was apparently published in the year 1526 after his death. Even this booklet has been lost, except for extracts quoted by Zwingli.

Conrad Grebel is not widely known and acclaimed like Luther and Zwingli, but his influence will live until the end of time in the lives of hundreds of thousands, both in the Mennonite Church and in other related movements. Without a commission from the state, without ordination from the church authorities, without benefit of theological training, with only the New Testament in his hands, and an abiding conviction that Christ meant that men should order their lives according to His teachings, Conrad Grebel challenged the world of his time. He gave his all to his faith, sacrificing an attractive career among men for the sake of the kingdom of God.

27

Felix Manz, c.1498-1527

Like Conrad Grebel, Felix Manz was a university student and the son of a good Zurich family; his father had been one of the clergy of the Zurich cathedral. From the beginning he was a follower of Zwingli but soon joined with Grebel and others in the demand for a thorough reformation. Meetings of the Brethren were held in his house in 1524, where he expounded the Old Testament from the original Hebrew, and the records make it clear that he was a leader with Grebel in the earliest days of the brotherhood. He was in prison several times in 1525 and 1526, but ceased not his preaching and baptizing in the territory around Zurich. In December, 1526, he was arrested for the last time and executed on January 5, 1527, by drowning in the Limmat River in Zurich as the first martyr of the Brethren at the hands of the Zwinglians. Eberli Bolt, who was burned at the stake on May 29, 1525, by the Catholic authorities of Schwyz, Switzerland, was the very first martyr of the Brethren, but he apparently was executed as a Protestant, not because he was one of the Brethren.

George Blaurock, c.1490-1529

Next to Conrad Grebel, George Blaurock was the most influential leader in the very beginning of the Mennonite Church in Switzerland. We know little of his origin except that he came from Bonaduz, a town in the eastern Alps. At the beginning of the evangelical movement he came to Zurich to converse with Zwingli. Finding that Zwingli, according to his understanding of the Gospel, did not follow the teachings of Christ, he turned to Conrad Grebel and his friends and decided that they were holding to the truth. Early in 1525 he joined them, took part in debates which were set for the defense of the faith in the year 1525, and suffered the persecution which all the Brethren had to face. He was of unusual ability as a speaker, and aggressive and courageous to an extreme. After exile from Zurich in January, 1527, he traveled about Switzerland preaching at various places, including Bern, Biel, and Appenzell, and finally in May, 1529, went to the Tyrol, just east of Switzerland. After four short months of effective ministry there he was burned at the stake at Clausen, on September 6, 1529. It is claimed that he preached to the crowd that witnessed his execution. Blaurock is largely responsible for the founding of the church in the Tyrol and Austria.

The summary of Blaurock's life and death as given in the *Martyrs' Mirror* is well worth noting. "About this time in the year 1529 was George Blaurock (after he had proclaimed and spread the truth for two or three years in Switzerland and especially in Tyrol in which he traveled, in order to be a source of salvation by his stewardship of his talent and by his zeal for the house of God), together with his companions, captured at Gufidaum and burned alive with fire not far from Clausen."

Michael Sattler, 1495-1527

One of the most attractive figures in the early history of the church is that of Michael Sattler, who was acclaimed even by his enemies as "a true friend of God." Formerly the prior of a monastery in the Black Forest, and a well-educated man, Sattler knew the Scriptures in the original languages. He was attracted to Zurich by the teachings of the Brethren in the year 1525, and being found among them was arrested and exiled from Zurich. He must have been baptized as a member of the group, for shortly thereafter we find him on an itinerant ministry throughout southwestern Germany, including the cities of Strasburg and Horb. A pastoral letter to the congregation at Horb reveals him to be a man of deep piety and warm love for the church. It is believed that he called together a conference of leaders of the church in February, 1527, at a place called Schleitheim, not far from Schaffhausen on the Rhine on the Swiss border. That conference is known to have prepared and published a confession of faith called "The Seven Articles of Schleitheim," which is the earliest known Mennonite confession of faith. Sattler was probably its author.

Three short months after this conference Sattler was arrested, condemned, and burned at the stake in Rottenburg after grievous torture. The record of his suffering and death, and his testimony to the church, have been preserved and published. It is one of the most moving stories of martyrdom and faithfulness in the early history of the church. Thus Sattler's influence has extended far beyond the two short years of his ministry in the early days of the Brethren.

Pilgram Marpeck, c.1495-1556

One of the most unusual men among the early leaders of the Anabaptist Brethren in Switzerland and South Germany was a mining engineer named Pilgram Marpeck. Born at Rattenberg in the Tyrol, Marpeck was well trained in the schools of his day, and early distinguished himself as a mining engineer in his home country. He was elected to the City Council of his home town in 1523, and by 1525 was a mine magistrate.

He was converted to Lutheranism in 1526, but in another year found that the Swiss Brethren were more true to the Scriptures and cast his lot with them. In 1528 he was made to suffer greatly because of his faith, being expelled from his position and suffering confiscation of his property. He fled for refuge to the city of Strasburg, where he served for several years as a distinguished engineer in the employ of the city. At the same time, being active in preaching and testifying to his faith, he began to baptize converts and organized a church. Banished from the city of Strasburg in 1532 he later found his way to Augsburg, where he spent the last years of his life, serving from 1544 to his death in 1556 as an engineer in the employ of the city.

Marpeck was an able leader and writer. At least three books written by him have been preserved, one of 1542 entitled *Admonition,* a treatise on baptism and the Lord's Supper, a second of 1544 entitled *An Explanation of the Testament,* and a third written about the same time, a large volume entitled *Vindication.* These three volumes are the most extensive source material for the teaching of the early Swiss Brethren, and may still be read with profit. Marpeck, the only one of the Swiss leaders to be allowed an extensive career in the church, may be considered the "Menno Simons of the South" in terms of his influence and significance.

CHAPTER 5

The Founding of the Dutch Mennonite Brotherhood

The seed of the Mennonite faith had been sown in Northwest Germany and Holland in the year 1530, first in the city of Emden, then in the city of Amsterdam, and from there throughout all of the Low Countries. Unfortunately the man who scattered the seed through this territory became sadly confused in his understanding of the nature of the Gospel of the church, and so combined with the true ideals of the Swiss Brethren some fanatical notions about the establishment of an earthly kingdom of God. This man was Melchior Hofmann (1495-1543), at first a Lutheran lay-preacher, in 1530 an Anabaptist in Strasburg, then a wandering Anabaptist preacher for a few years, who ended his life in a ten-year imprisonment in Strasburg in 1543. Because of Hofmann's fanaticism, much confusion existed in the minds of his followers for the five years after 1530. Gradually, however, the atmosphere cleared, and two parties developed out of the confusion. One was the radical revolutionary party which captured the majority of Hofmann's followers and perverted the whole movement into a dreadful enterprise to establish the kingdom of God on earth by force. These men, led by a certain John of Leiden and a certain John Matthys, finally were able to get control of the city of Münster in Northwest Germany in the year 1534, where they established their "kingdom" and remained in power for a short period of time. In the following year, however, they were completely overthrown by the rightful authorities of that territory, and the movement was wiped out. Meanwhile the other party, the minority of Hofmann's followers who had refused to go along with John of Leiden and his radicals, remained as a body of peaceful Brethren holding very similar doctrines to those of the Swiss Brethren, their spiritual ancestors. This group was organized in the year 1533, two years before the tragedy at Münster, under the leadership of two able brothers, Obbe and Dirk Philips, who lived at that time in the city of Leeuwar-

31

den in Friesland, the northwest corner of Holland. These brethren, who came to be known as Obbenites, were horror-stricken at the outcome of the revolutionary Hofmannite faction, and were more than ever convinced that the peaceful, Scriptural Anabaptist faith as espoused by them was the true way of God. This group of Obbenites was the beginning of the Dutch Mennonite movement.

Until the Münsterite movement had spent its force, the Obbenites made slow progress. However, when it became evident to all that Münsterism was an utter failure, hundreds of earnest but misguided Christians were glad to return to the true Christian way. In the year 1536 and after there was a rapid growth of the Obbenite group throughout all of Northwest Germany and Holland which revealed that it was destined to become a great and powerful movement, even more powerful than the movement of the Swiss Brethren which began in Zurich in 1525.

Before we trace the further history of this group, let us compare it to the Brethren in Switzerland. In all basic doctrines and practices the two groups were identical. Both held to the Holy Scriptures as the sole authority for faith and life, both desired a church composed of believers only, and both insisted upon a genuine life of Christian holiness and obedience to the Word of God. Since, however, there was no direct connection between the Swiss Brethren and the Obbenites, except for the slender roundabout connection through Melchior Hofmann, we must believe that the Obbenites and Swiss Brethren achieved a common faith because they both found their doctrines in a simple acceptance of the New Testament. The history of the Swiss Brethren in the early years is more clear and consistent, whereas the history of the early years of the Obbenite movement is more confused and uncertain. However, once the Obbenites found their way through the confusion of the times, and once they acquired able and strong leadership, they were equally as effective, if not more so, in the spreading of the true Gospel and the establishment of a New Testament church, as were the Swiss Brethren in their time and place. Today descendants of both the Swiss and the Dutch branches of the Mennonite Church find themselves in hearty agreement on all the fundamental tenets of faith and practices of the Gospel.

In the year 1536 the Obbenites won to their cause a very able Catholic priest, who was at that time serving in the parish of Witmarsum, Friesland, only about thirty miles from Leeuwarden. This priest, named Menno Simons, who was baptized by Obbe Philips in the year 1536, shortly afterward was persuaded to accept ordination as an elder or bishop, and from that time on became the outstanding leader of the group. Soon after this Obbe Philips made a tragic decision. He turned his back upon the faith which he had first espoused and disappeared from the movement. His brother, Dirk Philips, remained an outstanding leader in the group until his death in 1568.

Because it was soon clear to all that Menno Simons was the outstanding leader of the group, people gradually began to name the group after Menno, first using the name "Menist" about the year 1545, later changed to "Mennonite." This is the origin of the name of the Mennonite Church. Since Menno Simons' writings were numerous and powerful, and since he soon became the most widely known figure of the whole movement, writers and historians generally came to call both the Swiss and the Dutch Brethren after his name. Later, however, the Dutch Mennonites preferred to call themselves "Doopsgezinde," in German "Taufgesinnte," which translated into English would be something like "Baptism-minded." Accordingly today the followers of Menno in his own native land of Holland are no longer called Mennonites, whereas his followers in Germany, and the descendants of the Swiss Brethren, are the ones who call themselves Mennonites.

The story of the expansion of the early Mennonite movement into Holland and North Germany is a thrilling one. Menno, although a price was early placed upon his head, traveled and labored unceasingly throughout Holland and northern Germany from Amsterdam to Leeuwarden, to Groningen, to Emden, to Cologne, to Lübeck, and according to tradition, up the Baltic coast as far as Danzig. He was particularly influential through his writings, a total of twenty-four titles being published from the year 1539 to 1561 under his name. Several of these were extensive books. One of them, entitled *The Foundation,* became very popular and was a powerful force in spreading the faith of the Mennonite Church. Menno was a good leader, and was looked up to by his brethren as the father of the church until his death at his home in Wuestenfelde near Lübeck in 1561.

But the founding of the church in many places in Holland and northwestern Germany was due as much to Menno's colaborers as it was to himself. Dirk Philips early served the territory from Lübeck eastward, making Danzig his headquarters. The church in Danzig, which is still in existence, was apparently founded by him. Another very able leader was Leonard Bouwens, who was ordained in 1546 as minister and 1551 as elder and was in charge of the territory in Holland. A third able leader was Gillis of Aachen, who was ordained in 1542 to serve the territory around Cologne.

The strongest growth of the movement was in northwestern Holland in the province of Friesland, where very early a large portion of the population were converted and baptized into the Mennonite Church. However, strong churches were also established around Amsterdam, Haarlem, and Rotterdam, and on down into the territory of Flanders. From 1540 to 1570 the Mennonite movement was the strongest Protestant movement in the whole Low Countries. It was not until later that the Calvinist movement outdistanced it.

In Holland, as in Switzerland, the Catholic authorities persecuted the new movement thoroughly. Hundreds of martyrs lost their lives, and thousands were persecuted with imprisonment, torture, and exile. The persecution in Flanders was so severe that except for those who fled into Holland, few of the brethren survived. Because of the harsh rule of the Catholic overlords of Holland, who were at that time Spanish, a revolt broke out soon after the middle of the sixteenth century, which led to a long and bitter war, though it finally brought the independence of Holland. The leaders of this war of independence were Protestants to a large extent, and since they themselves were persecuted, they were more inclined to be tolerant of the Mennonites, even though the latter as nonresistants did not take part in the war. This measure of toleration enabled the Mennonite Church in Holland to maintain itself in spite of earlier persecution. In the latter part of the century it prospered greatly, whereas the Mennonite movement in South Germany and Switzerland was almost exterminated at about the same time.

CHAPTER 6

Early Dutch Mennonite Leaders

The early leaders of the Mennonite Church in Holland are more widely known than those in Switzerland. Whereas Conrad Grebel, Pilgram Marpeck, and Michael Sattler are less known names among us today, Menno Simons is a household name, known even outside the bounds of the church. He has been supposed by many to be the founder of the Mennonite Church, but it is clear from the preceding chapters of this book, that this is not the case. Menno joined the church eleven years after its beginning in Switzerland, he never lived in Switzerland, his writings were not available in German until the year 1575, and he differed in certain points on theology and church discipline from the Swiss Brethren. Nevertheless, he is one of the great leaders of the church, and deserves full credit for his able and devoted service in the earliest days of the brotherhood.

Menno Simons, 1496-1561

Menno Simons was born in the little town of Witmarsum, a few miles from the North Sea in Friesland, Holland. He came from a peasant family, but, being set apart for the Catholic priesthood, received the usual training for that office and by 1524 entered upon his career in the church. For twelve years he served as parish priest, 1524-36, first for seven years in the town of Pingjum and then for five years in his home town of Witmarsum.

Even though Menno Simons was a Catholic priest, he himself testifies that he knew nothing of the Bible until years after he was in the service of the church. He was a typical priest of his time, performing the duties of his office which consisted of the conduct of the service of worship called the mass, baptizing children, hearing confessions, and caring for his parish, but indulging in the common

35

amusements of card playing and drinking, and failing to take life very seriously.

The story of Menno Simons' conversion as told by himself in his own writings is an interesting one. It was not a sudden conversion, but one that finally came with overwhelming power at the end of a long period of struggle. The struggle began in the very first year of his service as a priest in 1525, when he began to doubt that the bread and wine of the mass were actually changed into the body and blood of the Lord. Tormented by doubts on this point he finally decided to seek help in the New Testament. He had never read the Bible before, since he accepted the teaching that the church was infallible and the Bible was not necessary. But once having decided to read the Bible he was inevitably led to a conversion experience and a complete break with the Catholic Church. He found, of course, that the New Testament does not teach the Catholic doctrine of transformation of the bread and the wine of the communion into the body and blood of Christ, and when he discovered this, he was forced to decide either for the Scriptures or for the church. He decided for the Scriptures. This did not lead to an immediate break with the church or to a full experience of conversion, even though it came after practically four years of struggle. It was not long until he was led to doubt another major pillar of the church, namely, the doctrine of infant baptism. He was led to this experience by learning of one of the "brethren," a man named Sicke Freerks, who was executed in 1531 in the city of Leeuwarden because he had been baptized the second time. Again Menno sought the answer to his doubts about baptism in the Scriptures, and again he found that the Catholic doctrine was not taught in the New Testament.

But it was another four years until Menno came to the final decision in the break with the church. This decision was brought about when Menno saw the grievous damage that was done by the revolutionary doctrines of John Matthys and the Münsterites who had succeeded in misleading hundreds in the immediate vicinity of Witmarsum. A band of these poor people, thinking that they too could help to establish a kingdom of God on earth, had been involved in a brief battle with the authorities in which most of them were slaughtered. When Menno Simons saw how these poor "sheep without a shepherd" had been willing to die in endeavoring to find the true faith, while he himself was continuing a life of ease and pleasure unwilling to stand for his faith, he was deeply convicted in his soul. Finally about April,

1535, he surrendered to God, and pledged his life henceforth to the Gospel.

Shortly thereafter he found his way to the Obbenite group in Leeuwarden, where he was baptized in January, 1536. As related earlier, he accepted the call to serve as an elder or bishop, receiving ordination to this office at the hands of Obbe Philips in 1536. He at once gave himself unreservedly to the shepherding of the brethren, to the defense of the Gospel, and to the preaching of the faith to all men. He used his gifts of writing effectively and became widely known through his books.

The following extracts of Menno Simons' own writing effectively describe his experience of conversion and his call to service.

"Behold thus, my reader, the God of mercy, through His abounding grace which He bestowed upon me, a miserable sinner, has first touched my heart, given me a new mind, humbled me in His fear, taught me in part to know myself, turned me from the way of death and graciously called me into the narrow path of life, into the communion of His saints. To Him be praise forevermore. Amen."

"When I heard this [the call] my heart was greatly troubled. Apprehension and fear was on every side. For on the one hand I saw my limited talents, my great lack of knowledge, the weakness of my nature, the timidity of my flesh, the very great wickedness, wantonness, perversity and tyranny of the world, the mighty great sects [the persecuting state churches], the subtlety of many men, and the indescribably heavy cross which, if I began to preach, would be the more felt; and on the other hand I recognized the pitifully great hunger, want, and need of the God-fearing, pious souls, for I saw plainly that they erred as innocent sheep which have no shepherd.

"When the persons before mentioned did not desist from their entreaties, and my own conscience made me uneasy in view of the great hunger and need already spoken of, I consecrated myself, soul and body, to the Lord, and committed myself to His gracious leading, and I began in due time [i.e., after having been ordained to the ministry of the Word] according to His holy Word to teach and to baptize, to labor with my limited talents in the harvest field of the Lord, to assist in building up His holy city and temple and to repair the dilapidated walls."

For the remaining twenty-five years of his life Menno lived the life of an itinerant evangelist and bishop, fleeing from place to place to find refuge. A price of two thousand guilders had been placed upon his head, but he was able to escape his enemies and lived to die a natural death in 1561 after twenty-five years of service.

From 1536 until 1543 Menno labored in Holland, spending the years 1541 to 1543 in and about Amsterdam. During these years he published seven books and booklets. From 1543 until 1546 he labored faithfully in Northwest Germany in the neighborhood of Emden and Cologne. From 1546 until his death in 1561 he had his headquarters in Holstein, first at Wismar on the Baltic, and later in a small town between Hamburg and Lübeck called Wuestenfelde. The last years of his life he spent in relative peace, since the Count of Ahlefeld, on whose land he settled, tolerated and protected Menno and permitted him to establish a small print shop in his home. From this print shop many additional booklets were published and new editions of his older books were printed.

Menno Simons is undoubtedly the greatest figure in the history of the Mennonite Church. He had a sane and balanced program emphasizing both a sound faith and a sound life. He was a fearless leader and a capable organizer. In thorough loyalty to the Word of God, he labored unceasingly for the establishment of true Christianity among men.

Dirk Philips, 1504-68

Little is known of Dirk Philips, except that he was born in Leeuwarden, Holland, in 1504, was an able co-worker of Menno Simons, and the writer of an influential book called *Enchiridion*. With his brother, Obbe Philips, he was one of the cofounders of the church in Holland, being numbered in the little group in 1533 in Leeuwarden who took their stand against the fanaticism of the followers of Melchior Hofmann. He was ordained as an elder in the church and served the territory from Lübeck eastward along the Baltic. He settled in the city of Danzig and was the first bishop of the church in that city, where he died in 1568.

Leonard Bouwens, 1515-82

Leonard Bouwens was born at Sommelsdyk in the Netherlands in 1515. As a youth he was active in political affairs and was known as an orator. He was converted to the Mennonite Church and ordained a minister in 1546, being further ordained as elder by Menno Simons himself in 1551. Bouwens was the most able evangelist among the early leaders, being active for over thirty years until his death in 1582. He kept a list of the converts baptized by him, which contains no less than 10,252 names. He was a good leader and a capable bishop, serving the congregations in Holland.

Other leaders of the Mennonites of Holland served faithfully, among whom was Gillis of Aachen, who was born about 1500 and served the churches in the vicinity of Cologne. He was ordained as bishop by Menno Simons in 1542. In 1557, after fifteen years of faithful service, he was arrested for his faith near Antwerp and, losing courage, recanted. He was, nevertheless, beheaded by the authorities in spite of his tragic surrender.

No doubt many others might be named, but the great trio of Menno Simons, Dirk Philips, and Leonard Bouwens will remain the outstanding leaders of the early Dutch Mennonite Church. They were the men who carried the banner in those critical days, and who built a strong organization with numerous active congregations and thousands of members.

CHAPTER 7

Foundation Stones of the Mennonite Faith

The goal which our forefathers in Switzerland and Holland set for themselves was the highest possible goal for Christians. It was, to revive original New Testament Christianity. Historians of the state churches are convinced that this was the purpose of the early Brethren. Professor Johann Loserth of Austria says: "More radically than any other movement for reform, the Anabaptists strove to follow the footsteps of the church of the first centuries and to renew unadulterated original Christianity."* Professor Gottfried Strasser of Switzerland says: "Despairing of the possibility of bringing the purity of the Christian life to realization among the broad masses, they aimed at establishing within the narrower limits of those who took the Christian life more seriously, a true Christian church of those who were striving for active holiness according to the example of the apostolic church." Professor Max Goebel of Germany says: "The essential and distinguishing characteristic of this church is its great emphasis upon the actual personal conversion and regeneration of every Christian through the Holy Spirit. . . . They aimed with special emphasis at carrying out and realizing the Christian doctrine and faith in the heart and life of every Christian and in the whole Christian church. Their aim was the bringing together of all the true believers out of the great degenerated national churches into a true Christian church. That which the Reformation was originally intended to accomplish they aimed to bring into full immediate realization." Abraham Hulshof, a Dutch Mennonite historian, says: "The Anabaptist aim was a church of those who took their Christian profession seriously, who were in real earnest in the endeavor to conform their lives to the requirements of the Gospel. They aimed to form voluntary congre-

---

* For most of the quotations in this section the author is indebted to John Horsch, *Mennonites in Europe* (Scottdale, 1942).

40

gations of those who believed and were truly converted. Their aim was to constitute in the midst of the world a living church of Christ that was separated from the world and was following Him in brotherly unison."

In short, that which Martin Luther and the other Protestant reformers had first intended but later surrendered, namely, a complete reformation of the church according to the New Testament pattern, this the Brethren actually carried through. Where Luther and Zwingli compromised, they made no compromise. For them it was all of Christ and all of His teachings or none. They did not pay the price of diluting the Gospel in order to establish a great institution within which to shepherd the entire population, but they were willing to pay and did pay the necessary price to have the whole truth of God and to bring it into full realization in the experience of all true Christians.

The New Testament pattern of Christianity, as the Brethren saw it, required more than the experience of forgiveness of sins through justification by faith in Christ. It required a genuine change of life, a newness of living, which was true holiness in full obedience to Christ. This demand for "holiness of life," that is, for real "life," was the great central foundation stone of the faith of the Brethren. It is still the central stone in the house of our Mennonite faith today. In the great debate held in 1532 at Zofingen, Switzerland, between the Brethren and the Reformed Church, the spokesmen of the Brethren said: "In the early church only those were received as members who were converted through repentance to newness of life. The true church is conformed to the nature of Christ." In another similar great debate in 1538 in Berne, a spokesman of the Brethren said:

While yet in the national church, we obtained much instruction from the writings of Luther, Zwingli, and others, concerning the mass and other papal ceremonies, that they are vain. Yet we recognized a great lack as regards repentance, conversion, and the true Christian life. Upon these things my mind was bent. I waited and hoped for a year or two, since the minister had much to say of amendment of life, of giving to the poor, loving one another, and abstaining from evil. But I could not close my eyes to the fact that the doctrine which was preached and which was based on the Word of God was not carried out. No beginning was made toward true Christian living, and there was no unison in the teaching concerning the things that were necessary. And although the mass and the images were finally abolished, true repentance and Christian love were not in evidence. Changes were made only as concerned external things. This gave me occasion to inquire further into these matters. Then God sent His messengers, Conrad Grebel and others, with whom I conferred about the fundamental teachings of the apostles and the Christian life and practice. I found them men who had surrendered themselves to the doctrine of Christ by "Buss-fertigkeit" [repentance evidenced by fruits]. With their assistance we established a congregation in which repentance was in evidence by newness of life in Christ.

"In evidence" is the keynote which rings through these striking testimonies of the early Swiss Brethren. Among the followers of Luther and Zwingli, they believed, repentance, conversion, love, and the true Christian life were not *in evidence*. Among the Brethren the goal was that the inward experience of repentance and conversion should be *in evidence* by a newness of life in Christ. The whole of life was to be under the lordship of Christ. The medieval mystics and men like Brother Lawrence insisted upon "The Practice of the Presence of God" within, but Conrad Grebel, Menno Simons, and their associates insisted upon the practice of the presence of Christ *in action.* They interpreted the Christian life to be not so much the inward experience of the grace of God, as Luther did, but the outward application of that grace to all human conduct, and the consequent Christianization of all human relationships.

This central truth of newness of life and applied Christianity created a new type of church and Christian society among the Brethren. In describing this church and society we come to the subsidiary foundation stones of the faith.

First, there is the concept of the nature of the church as a fellowship of true believers. Menno Simons said: "Christ's church consists of the chosen of God, His saints and beloved who have washed their robes in the blood of the Lamb, who are born of God and led by Christ's spirit, who are in Christ and Christ in them, who hear and believe His word, live in their weakness according to His commandments, and in patience and meekness follow in His footsteps." The church was to be composed of believers only, who voluntarily assumed the Christian life and pledged their lives to Christ in deed and in truth. Voluntary church membership, based upon conversion, and involving a commitment to holy living, this was the heart of their concept of the church. It is a principle which is widely accepted today among American Protestants, but it must be remembered that it was the unique and original creation of the Brethren in Reformation times who held this view in opposition to the prevailing views of the time, and who suffered persecution for it.

The Reformers, on the other hand, adopted the principle of the mass church, with compulsory membership by law and force, effected through infant baptism of the entire population. They knew well that such a church was not the true church of Christ, but they hoped that the testimony of true Christians within the church would leaven the great mass. Whereas the Brethren insisted on discipline and the maintenance of the Gospel standard and active participation in church life as a condition of continued membership in the church, the state churches could not possibly exercise such discipline and secure active participation. Since infant baptism was the only guarantee of the establishment of the mass church, on the one hand, and believers' baptism was the only guarantee of the establishment of the true church, on the other hand, baptism became the crucial point of conflict between the Reformers and the Brethren. Yet it is clear that this point was not the real issue, but only the outward symbol of it.

Another foundation stone was the concept of the nonconformity of the church to the world. Since Christians were to live in newness of life, there would of necessity be a radical difference between them and the world, and separation of the two ways of life was inevitable. The world would not tolerate the practice of Christian principles in society in general, and the church could not tolerate the practice of worldly ways of life within its membership; hence the only way out was separation, the gathering of true Christians into their own Christian society, where Christ's way was practiced. On this principle of separation Menno Simons says: "The whole evangelical Scriptures teach that Christ's church was and must be a people separated from the world in doctrine, life, and worship." In the great debate of 1528 at Zofingen spokesmen of the Swiss Brethren said: "The true church is separated from the world and is conformed to the nature of Christ. If the church is yet at one with the world, we cannot recognize it as the true church."

Another foundation stone was the insistence on the practice of true brotherhood and love among the members of the church. This principle was understood to mean not just the expression of pious sentiments, but the actual practice of sharing possessions to meet the needs of others in the spirit of true mutual aid. Hans Leopold, a Swiss Brethren martyr of 1528, said of the Brethren: "If they know of any one who is in need, whether or not he is a member of their church, they believe it their duty, out of love to God, to render him help and aid." Heinrich Seiler, a Swiss Brethren martyr of 1535, said "I do not believe it wrong that a Christian has property of his own, but yet he is nothing more than a steward." An early Hutterian book states that one of the questions addressed by the Swiss Brethren to applicants for baptism was: "Whether they consecrated themselves with all their temporal possessions to the service of God and His people." A Protestant of Strasburg, visitor at a Swiss Brethren baptismal service in that city in 1557, reported that a question addressed to applicants for baptism was: "Whether they, if necessity required it, would devote all their possessions to the service of the brotherhood, and would not fail any member that is in need, if they were able to render aid." Heinrich Bullinger, successor to Zwingli as leader of the Reformed Church in Zurich, a bitter enemy of the Brethren, states: "They teach that every good Christian is under duty before God from motives of love, to use, if need be, all his possessions to supply the necessities of life to any of the brethren who are in need."

This principle of full brotherhood and stewardship, of sincere practice of mutual aid, was truly a foundation stone of the faith of our forefathers. It was actually practiced, and not just speculatively considered. In its absolute form it became the way of life for the Hutterian brotherhood and has remained so ever since. What a different world this would be, if Christian Europe, from Reformation times to the present, had accepted the way of brotherhood and stewardship in material possessions which our forefathers proposed and practiced. What a tragedy that some Mennonites have abandoned the spirit and practice of this great principle.

Another great foundation stone was the principle of peace, love, and nonresistance as applied to all human relationships. The Brethren understood this to mean complete abandonment of the principle of war and violence, and of the taking of human life. Conrad Grebel said in 1524: "True Christians use neither the worldly sword nor engage in war, since among them taking human life has ceased entirely, for we are no longer under the Old Covenant. . . . The Gospel and those who accept it are not to be protected with the sword, neither should they thus protect themselves." Pilgram Marpeck in 1544, speaking of Matthew 5, said: "All bodily, worldly, carnal, earthly fighting, conflicts, and wars are annulled and abolished among them through such law." Menno Simons wrote: "The regenerated do not go to war, nor engage in strife. They are the children of peace who have beaten their swords into plowshares and their spears into pruning hooks, and know of no war. . . . Spears and swords of iron we leave to those who, alas, consider human blood and swine's blood of well-nigh equal value." In this principle of nonresistance, which was thoroughly believed and resolutely practiced by all the Brethren throughout Europe from the beginning until the last century, our forefathers were again creative leaders, far ahead of their times, antedating the Quakers in this by over one hundred years. They held this principle in a day when not only both Catholic and Protestant churches endorsed war as an instrument in political affairs, but used it in religious combat. It is obvious that a church which would kill individual dissenters of a godly life such as the Anabaptists would not hesitate to use the force of armies to exterminate other churches.

Space will permit only the bare mention of two other great foundation stones: the separation of church and state, which was the inevitable outcome of the conception of the church and the doctrine of nonresistance held by the Brethren; and the principle of freedom of conscience. In both these principles the Brethren were again creative pioneers, far ahead of their time. Freedom of conscience became widespread only after the French Revolution and the Napoleonic wars, that is, in the nineteenth century. But three hundred years before, according to Bullinger, the Swiss Brethren taught: "One cannot and should not use force to compel anyone to accept the faith, for faith is a free gift of God. It is wrong to compel any one by force or coercion to embrace the faith, or to put to death anyone for the sake of his erring faith. It is an error that in the church any sword other than that of the divine Word should be used. The secular kingdom should be separated from the church, and no secular ruler should exercise authority in the church. The Lord has commanded simply to preach the Gospel, and not to compel any one by force to accept it. . . . The true church of Christ has the characteristic that it suffers or endures persecution but does not inflict persecution upon any one." Bullinger reports these statements not in commendation of the Brethren but in condemnation of them, though he has thereby rendered history a great service by recording the views of the Swiss Brethren on liberty of conscience. He condemns these views as erroneous, urging the need of severest persecution against those who hold such "heretical views," and after quoting the Brethren, attempts to refute their position point by point, closing with the assertion that to put to death Anabaptists is a necessary and commendable service.

Similar statements could be quoted from all the leading Reformers.

Were there space to do so, the application of the foundation stones of the Mennonite faith could be traced into various areas of life and experience, such as simplicity of life and spirit, nonswearing of oaths, and concrete applications of nonconformity to the world, but sufficient has been given to show what the foundations of the faith of the early Swiss and Dutch Brethren were.

As we survey the faith of the Swiss and Dutch Brethren, we are well-nigh overwhelmed by its tremendous breadth and depth. What magnificent creative conceptions, taken from the very heart of the Gospel! What great faith they must have had to espouse these principles, and what grace and power they had from God to live them in the face of the bitterest persecution! They challenged the world of their day to the utmost, not only the pagan world, but the Christian world of their time and of all times. If ever there was a wholehearted and uncompromising attempt to establish the kingdom of God on earth, it was the endeavor of our forefathers of the sixteenth century. They failed to win the world for their program; the number of their followers after the winnowing of persecution was small; and they and their descendants, particularly their descendants of later times, were imperfect and often failed; but they had caught the vision of a new heaven and new earth in which dwelleth righteousness and in which the Lamb is the light thereof, and for this they gave the full measure of devotion. The greatest tragedy of modern Mennonitism round the world has been, not that some of us have failed to achieve the vision, but that many of us have surrendered the vision altogether.

CHAPTER 8

The Price of Faith:
Persecution and Martyrdom

From its very beginning the Church of Jesus Christ suffered persecution. In fact, Jesus promised this to His followers, for as He told them, if the world hated Him, it would also hate them. But He told them also: "Be of good cheer, I have overcome the world." Beginning with Stephen, thousands, yes, many thousands, suffered and died in glorious victory for their faith, happy to die for the One who had died for them. The height of this persecution came in the third century when the Roman Empire tried with all the means at its disposal to exterminate the church but failed. Even the very severity of the persecution may have contributed to this failure, for the steadfastness of the martyrs and their joyful death under great suffering was a powerful testimony. Tertullian, one of the early church fathers, uttered a great truth when he said about the year 200, "The blood of the martyrs is the seed of the church." So it has always been.

But if the pagan persecution of the early church was severe, the persecution of the Anabaptist-Mennonites by the Catholic and Protestant state churches of Reformation times was, in proportion to numbers, still more severe. Recent church historians testify to the bloody character of this persecution. In the first ten years over five thousand of the Swiss Brethren were executed in Switzerland and surrounding territories, particularly in Austria and the Tyrol. Within the first five years, most of the early leaders died at the stake, under the headsman's ax, or by drowning. Persecution set in immediately upon the organization of the church in 1525, and although the last martyr in Switzerland was executed in 1614, Bernese Mennonites were being sold as galley slaves as late as 1750. Full toleration for Swiss Mennonites did not come until 1815. And late into the eighteenth century Hutterian Brethren were still being executed in the territory of Transylvania and Hungary. In Holland toleration came somewhat earlier, though not formally and fully until 1798. The last execution there took place in 1574.

This persecution of our forefathers, both in Switzerland and Holland, was no unorganized lynching by riotous mobs; it was the settled and legal policy of governmental authorities. The first death sentences were imposed in 1525, and by 1527 Anabaptism was a capital crime in several Swiss cantons and in Austria and Bavaria. On January 4, 1528, Emperor Charles V of Germany issued a general mandate against the Anabaptists, which was to be read from all pulpits of all cities, towns, and villages in the empire, decreeing that not only those who had received baptism, but all parents who did not have their children baptized, should be guilty of a crime deserving death. When it became evident that the issuance of this and similar decrees had no great effect, and that all efforts to halt the spread of the movement proved vain, the authorities resorted to desperate measures. Armed executioners and mounted soldiers were sent in companies throughout the land to hunt down the Anabaptists and kill them on the spot without trial or sentence. Those who were overtaken on the highways or fields were killed with the sword, while those caught in their houses were often hanged to their doorposts or burned to death with their homes. In the year 1528, in the province of Swabia, four hundred mounted police were sent out to hunt down and exterminate the Anabaptists of the province. This number was later increased to eight hundred and finally to one thousand.

Enormous numbers were slaughtered, since it was comparatively easy to determine who was an Anabaptist by the simple expedient of asking him point blank. An Anabaptist disdained to save his life by telling an untruth and concealing his identity. On Christmas Day, 1531, an imperial provost named Berthold Aichele drove seventeen men and women into a farmhouse near Aalen in Württemberg and burned the building over their heads. Three hundred and fifty Anabaptists were executed in the Palatinate before 1530. The Count of Alzey of that province, after having put many to death, was heard to exclaim: "What shall I do? The more I kill, the greater becomes their number." At Ensisheim, the "slaughterhouse of Alsace," six hundred were killed in a few years. In the small town of Kitzbühel in the Tyrol sixty-eight were executed in one year. Two hundred and ten were burned at the stake in the valley of the Inn River in Austria. In the Tyrol and Gorizia it is estimated that one thousand were martyred by the end of 1531. In Holland, at least one thousand five hundred were executed. The Hutterian Chronicle records the execution of over two thousand.

In April, 1529, the imperial parliament of the German Empire, meeting at Spires, Germany, by imperial law passed a sentence of death upon all Anabaptists, decreeing that "every Anabaptist and rebaptized person of either sex shall be put to death by fire, sword, or some other way." Thus the cup of persecution was filled to the full. It is a marvel that any escaped. Still more marvelous is it that many were won to the faith by the steadfastness and joyful testimony of the martyrs. Many prayers, hymns, and admonitions of martyrs were addressed to the brotherhood from prison or delivered to the crowds at the scenes of execution. Numbers of these hymns and testimonies were preserved and published. More than one executioner faltered, according to the records, and refused to continue with his gruesome duty. In Switzerland in particular there was great sympathy among the common people for the persecuted Anabaptists, and frequently these sympathizers, sometimes called "Halfway-Anabaptists," gave open assistance to the persecuted ones. Accordingly decrees were passed punishing those who harbored Anabaptists, or gave any assistance to them. As late as 1551 the imperial parliament passed a decree ordering that judges and jurors who had scruples against pronouncing the death sentence upon anyone because of matters of faith should be removed from office and punished by heavy fines and imprisonment.

On the whole it must be said that the persecution accomplished its deadly purpose. What seemed destined in the providence of God to become a great popular movement sweeping over all Europe was completely exterminated in all of Middle and South Germany and Austria by 1600, and only a handful of Brethren were left in the back valleys and mountains of the Swiss Alps and surrounding Swiss territory. Only in Holland was the persecution unable to accomplish its purpose fully.

We are doubly challenged by these martyrs today. In the first place we are led to see that such a witness does have a power in the world, and in the second place we can see that no power on earth is strong enough to destroy faith in God. The most heroic examples of early Christian martyrdom were paralleled in the Anabaptist persecutions of Reformation times. Even their opponents admired the courage, fortitude, and patience of the Brethren. A contemporary Catholic writer said concerning the way in which Anabaptist martyrs met their death: "Such valiant dying has never been seen before, nor heard of except in the legends of the saints." The masses were impressed with the fact that the Anabaptists were in earnest in living the life that they professed. When Michael Hassel, after much suffering, died in the prison of Hohenwittling in Württemberg, the warden said: "If this man did not get to heaven, I shall despair of the courage even to knock at heaven's gate." The hangman of Burghausen, having beheaded three Anabaptists, exclaimed: "I should rather have executed seven thieves than these men. God have mercy." In 1549 a Mennonite martyr at Leeuwarden in Friesland was burned at the stake. Many people witnessing the execution exclaimed: "This was a good man; if he is not a Christian, there is no Christian in the whole world."

The inspiring record of the martyr deaths of thousands of Brethren, both men and women, together with many of their testimonies, has been preserved to become part of the devotional literature of the church. Many of the early hymns in both Swiss and Dutch hymnbooks such as the *Ausbund* (first published in 1564) were accounts of martyrdom or songs written by martyrs. As early as 1562 these accounts and testimonies were collected and published in Dutch in book form under the title, *Het Offer des Herrn (The Sacrifice of the Lord)*. Later this book was enlarged into what has become the most noteworthy book in all Mennonite literature, the *Martyrs' Mirror* of T. J. van Braght, first published in Holland in 1660. Another noteworthy book of this character was *Güldene Aepfel in silbernen Schalen (Golden Apples in Silver Bowls)*, first published in 1702, containing chiefly accounts of the martyrdom and testimonies of Michael Sattler (d. 1527) and Thomas von Imbroich (d. 1558). In books such as these we are compassed about with the great cloud of witnesses who counted not their lives precious, but died in faith having received the promise.

A fitting conclusion to this section is an inspiring description of Anabaptist persecutions written about 1542, taken from the Hutterian Chronicle, found at the close of a report of 2,173 brethren and sisters who gave their lives for their faith:

> No human being was able to take away out of their hearts what they had experienced, such zealous lovers of God were they. The fire of God burned within them. They would die the bitterest death, yea, they would die ten deaths rather than forsake the divine truth which they had espoused.
>
> They had drunk of the waters which had flowed from God's sanctuary, yea, the water of life. They realized that God helped them to bear the cross and to overcome the bitterness of death.

The fire of God burned within them. Their tent they had pitched not here upon earth, but in eternity, and of their faith they had a foundation and assurance. Their faith blossomed as a lily, their loyalty as a rose, their piety and sincerity as the flower of the garden of God. The angel of the Lord battled for them that they could not be deprived of the helmet of salvation. Therefore they have borne all torture and agony without fear. The things of this world they counted in their holy mind only as shadows, having the assurance of greater things. They were so drawn unto God that they knew nothing, sought nothing, desired nothing, loved nothing but God alone. Therefore they had more patience in their suffering than their enemies in tormenting them.

From the shedding of such innocent blood arose Christians everywhere, brothers all, for all this persecution did not take place without fruit. Many were moved thereby to give thought to these things, and to order their thinking and doing and living in the light of the future, so many indeed that finally the authorities in many places would no longer execute the martyrs publicly, as for instance in the Tyrol, but condemned and slew them secretly by night so that the people could not know of it.

In some places they literally filled the prisons and dungeons with them, as did the Count Palatine. The persecutors thought they could dampen and extinguish the fire of God. But the prisoners sang in their prisons and rejoiced so that the enemies outside became much more fearful than the prisoners and did not know what to do with them. Many others lay for years in dungeons and prisons and endured all sorts of pain and torture. Others had holes burned through their cheeks and were then let free.

The rest, who escaped all this, were driven from one land to another, from one town to the next. They had to be like owls and bitterns which dare not be seen by daylight. Often they had to hide away in rocks and cliffs, in wild forests, in caves and holes in the earth to save their lives. They were sought by catchpolls and dogs, were hunted and caught like birds. All were without guilt, without the least wicked deed, since they neither did nor desired to do any one the least harm or injury.

Everywhere they were cursed and slandered and lied about scandalously. It was said of them that they could bring people under their control by giving them to drink from a little flask. Scandalous lies were told about them, such as having their women in common. They were slandered devilishly as Anabaptists, seducers, rioters, fanatics. Everywhere were issued imperial, royal and princely mandates, decrees, and commands against them.

Many were talked to in wonderful ways, often day and night.

51

They were argued with, with great cunning and cleverness, with many sweet and smooth words, by monks and priests, by doctors of theology, with much false testimony, with threats and scolding and mockery, yea, with lies and grievous slanders against the brotherhood, but none of these things moved them or made them falter. Some sang praises to God while they lay in grievous imprisonment, as though they were in great joy. Some did the same as they were being led to the place of execution and death, singing joyfully with uplifted voice that it rang out loud. Others stepped to the place of death with a smile on their lips, praising that they were accounted worthy to die the death of the Christian hero, and would not have preferred even to die a natural death.

Note: The author is indebted to John Horsch, *Mennonites in Europe*, for much of the material in this chapter.

C. Experiences of European Mennonites to the Present

CHAPTER 9

The Hutterian Brethren and the Amish

The Hutterian Brethren

There is scarcely a story in all Christian history as moving as the story of the Hutterian Brethren, who for over four hundred years have maintained a Christian brotherhood based entirely on community ownership of all goods and the practice of brotherly love. Most Christians may not wish to accept their pattern of life, and few are willing to agree that complete Christian community of goods is commanded by the Scriptures, but none of us can deny the powerful testimony against the sin of selfishness and greed which the Hutterian way of life produces, nor the challenge to the highest devotion to the kingdom of God which arises out of their great history. When John Horsch wrote for the first time in English (1928) the story of their history, he called it a "Story of Martyrdom and Loyalty," and so it is. Other utopian societies have come and gone, but the Hutterians alone seem to have found the secret of perpetual brotherhood.

The Hutterian Brethren are an integral part of the Anabaptist-Mennonite movement, even though they have never borne the name "Mennonite." They differ from the Swiss Brethren, of whom they were originally a part, chiefly by their practice of "having all things common," which is, to be sure, a major difference. The origin of the group took place in the land of Moravia about 1528 in the midst of desperate need.

Moravia, a small territory lying north and east of Vienna, Austria, was more tolerant of Protestant "heretics" at first than other lands, even though it was nominally under the rule of the staunchly

Catholic Habsburg kings of Austria. Accordingly, Swiss Brethren, fleeing from persecution in their Swiss homeland as well as nearby regions, early found refuge here, particularly on the lands of the Lords of Liechtenstein near Nikolsburg. Even one of the Lords of Liechtenstein himself became a baptized member of the church which was organized there in 1526. Differences of opinion developed among the more than one thousand members at this place, which eventually led to a division, chiefly on the question of nonresistance. Those who were completely nonresistant were finally asked by the authorities to leave, and in the spring of the year 1528, between 200 and 300 persons, under the leadership of Jacob Widemann, moved farther eastward to Austerlitz, where they were invited to settle by the tolerant Lords von Kaunitz. Already in Nikolsburg the many penniless refugees made it necessary to practice a partial communism, but at Austerlitz it was still more necessary, since practically all were penniless refugees. The group chose "ministers of temporal needs," and according to the ancient Hutterian Chronicle, "the chosen men spread a cloak before the people, and every one laid down on it his earthly possessions, unconstrained and with a willing mind." Shortly after this another division occurred and the consistently communistic group moved on to nearby Auspitz. There the communistic Christian brotherhood, later called Hutterians after Jacob Hutter, their outstanding leader, was fully established, not by theory, but out of a deep sense of need and the response of Christian love to it.

It must be emphasized at the outset that Hutterian community of goods has nothing in common with modern materialistic communism, nor with humanitarian utopianism. The Hutterians do not believe that a communistic economic system will solve the ills of the world, nor do they believe that anyone without regard to his Christian faith can practice their way of life. For them, only children of God, blessed with the grace and power of God, can walk in this way. They do believe also that all true children of God will inevitably find this way to be the only right way.

The organization of the Hutterian brotherhood is the same today as it was appointed four hundred years ago by Jacob Hutter at Auspitz. A group of fifteen to twenty-five families form a community, called in German "Bruderhof," for which there is no good English translation. Each Bruderhof has a minister, that is, a religious leader, and a steward or supervisor who has charge of economic or business aspects of the life of the group. A body of four or five elders serve as a council of advisers and assistants to these men. All of these men are responsible to the congregation and remain in office only so long as they render satisfactory service. The steward is the business manager of the community. He directs the foremen who have charge of the various enterprises of the community, handles all the money, and does all the buying and selling. No money is in circulation in the community, no one is paid for labor or service, and no property is owned privately. Each Bruderhof is an independent, self-sustaining unit, not sharing ownership with the other Bruderhofs, though it gladly assists others by outright donations in time of need. All necessary economic activities for the production of food, clothing, and shelter are performed on the Bruderhof by its own members. All cultural activities are likewise provided within the Bruderhof, such as education and worship. The life on the Bruderhof is carried on in the spirit of true Christian simplicity and brotherhood, with the dominant ideal of full conformity to the will of God.

Hutterian history is an almost continuous story of persecution and martyrdom, more than is the case with any other Mennonite group. Jacob Hutter, who became their official leader in 1533, was executed in 1535. Until 1552 there was almost continuous persecution, forced by the Austrian rulers. The group fled from Moravia four times, twice to Hungary, only to come back each time. From 1552 to 1592 there was relative peace and quiet. In this time there was a remarkable growth, so that in Moravia and Hungary a total of at least fifty Bruderhofs, with possibly fifteen thousand souls, were established. Industries of all sorts developed among the Hutterians, to the great economic benefit of the entire land. Hutterian physicians served in noble courts, even in the court of the King of Bohemia. Many nobles had Hutterians for managers of their estates. The Hutterian school system became a model one. The Bruderhofs were outstanding examples of prosperity and progress.

In this period the Hutterians were aggressive in their missionary endeavors, sending out "apostles" throughout all Germany, who directed an almost constant stream of converts to the land of promise in Moravia and Hungary.

After 1593 a time of great tribulation set in which lasted for two hundred years and which brought the brotherhood almost to the point of extermination. In fact, by 1767 the entire group numbered only sixty-seven souls; but they were sixty-seven faithful and loyal souls, who kept the vision of brotherhood alive. During the time of tribulation the Brethren suffered from the Austro-Turkish War, the Thirty Years' War (1618-48), and the attempt of the government under Jesuit influence to wipe out the brotherhood entirely. They fled from Moravia to Hungary, then in 1621 to Transylvania, in 1767 to Rumania, and finally in 1770 to Russia. Within Russia they moved twice, and finally in 1874-80 the entire brotherhood migrated to South Dakota, near Freeman. After World War I, in which they suffered much persecution, most of the Bruderhofs moved to Manitoba and Alberta. More recently communities have been established in Saskatchewan, Ontario, Montana, North Dakota, and Washington, and there has been a sizable return to South Dakota. In 1963 they were living in about 120 communities or Bruderhofs, their Canadian membership numbering about 10,000 and that of the United States nearly 4,000. In rigidity of customs, and outward forms such as wearing of the beard and plain attire, they are similar to the Amish.

The Amish

The Amish are Mennonites, and strictly speaking should be called Amish Mennonites. They constitute the only major division among the Swiss Brethren, and separated late in history from this group. The break occurred in 1693, in the midst of bitter persecution, although endeavors to heal the schism delayed the absolute separation until 1697. It is encouraging to note that in Europe the division has been to all practical intents completely obliterated, and that in America within the past generation at least two thirds of the Amish group has again merged with the Mennonite body. Nevertheless there are still nineteen thousand baptized members of the main line of Amish in America, who with their children constitute a population of over forty thousand souls, the fourth largest Mennonite body in America.

Since the Amish in America will be treated in Part II, attention will be confined here to their origin and European history.

The cause of the division of 1693 was disagreement over strictness of discipline. Jacob Ammann, a young bishop probably from Alsace, led the party which desired to introduce the strict practice of avoidance of excommunicated members. In so doing he was following the teaching and practice of Menno Simons and Dirk Philips, together with most of the early Dutch Mennonites, but was going contrary to the practice of the Swiss Brethren, who had protested the strictness of Menno Simons' position, and who in conference in Strasburg in 1557 had refused to adopt this practice for their churches. The Dortrecht Confession of 1632 contains an article requiring avoidance, and since this confession was adopted by the churches of Alsace in 1660 as their own, it is probable that Dutch influence brought the innovation into some of the Swiss Brethren churches. The congregations in Switzerland have never adopted the Dortrecht Confession and never accepted avoidance. When the division finally came, most of the Alsace congregations, together with a minority of Swiss, followed Ammann, but most of the Swiss congregations, with a minority of Alsatians and all of the Palatinate congregations, followed Hans Reist, the older Swiss bishop whose leadership was accepted by the main body of the brethren. The common notion that forms of clothing or worship, or such minor points as "hooks and eyes" or the "beard," were the causes of the division is wholly erroneous. At the time of the division all the congregations on both sides followed common practices on these points. The difference today is due to the fact that the Amish churches have remained static on these points, while the Mennonite or "Reist" churches have "progressed" away from them.

The Amish congregations of America, most of which descend from settlers who came before the Revolutionary War (1738-56) or shortly after the Napoleonic wars (1817-50), have retained almost without change the forms of worship and church life that were in use among the Mennonites in Switzerland and Alsace two hundred and fifty years ago, having successfully resisted the influence of modern ways. Their challenge to the modern world should give us all pause to think whether in our acceptance of many changes and modern methods we may be in danger of losing some valuable elements from our heritage.

The Amish of 1697 have spread far and wide from their original home in Alsace. Large settlements were made in Zweibrücken (adjoining the Palatinate on the west and Alsace-Lorraine on the north), Montbeliard, just inside France some fifty miles southwest of Alsace, and Basel, Luxembourg, and Bavaria. In all of these places the Amish settlements still exist, but have lost their distinctiveness. Other settlements were made in Wittgenstein, Waldeck, and Hesse-Cassel, all of which have died out. A considerable settlement was made in Volhynia, Russia, in 1815, which later came to America. A portion of the large settlement made in Galicia in 1785 was also Amish. The major Amish settlements are now in America.

NOTE: The term *Amish* as it is used today applies exclusively to those Amish congregations which have steadfastly and successfully resisted change and still maintain the old ways of the forefathers in Europe and are accordingly known as the "Old Order Amish." The *Old Order Amish* number probably not more than one third of the descendants of the Amish who settled in America. The remainder have been absorbed in other more progressive groups. The following groups are Amish in origin: the Conservative Mennonites, the Beachy Amish, the Evangelical Mennonites, the Central Conference (now a part of the General Conference), and the majority of the (old) Mennonites west of Pennsylvania.

CHAPTER 10

The Expansion into Germany

a. Swiss Mennonites in South Germany and Their Experiences to 1914

Mennonitism began in Switzerland, and there it has continued to the present day. In the valley of the Emme River in the Canton of Berne not far from the Swiss capital there are still Mennonite congregations and Mennonite families which trace their origin back to the founding days of the church. The oldest of these dates from 1528. A few families have also persisted from the very beginning in the neighborhood of Basel, but the heart of Swiss Mennonitism has been the congregations in Berne. All other congregations in Switzerland were extinguished, either by persecution or emigration. Many congregations, some of them very large, had also been established in earliest times in all the German-speaking territory around Switzerland to the east and north, in Tyrol, Austria, Bavaria, Swabia, Alsace, the Palatinate, Franconia, down the Rhine Valley to Cologne, and in Hesse. In fact, by the middle of the sixteenth century the center of gravity of the movement was in South Germany. In 1557 a great conference of leaders was held in Strasburg, at which over fifty elders were present representing "more than fifty churches from the Eiffel (on the Luxembourg border) to Moravia, some with over five hundred members." By the year 1600 bloody presecution had exterminated all these churches. Few if any families survived. Had it not been for the Swiss churches the entire movement would have died out.

However, through emigration in the seventeenth century the Swiss Mennonites again spread into the territories north of Switzerland from which they had been exterminated, and today there are once again more than forty congregations of Mennonites in South Germany (the Palatinate, Hesse, Baden, Württemberg, Bavaria) with a total population, including unbaptized children, of about 5,500. This emigration from Switzerland was both forced and voluntary.

The severe persecution in Berne in the seventeenth century included torture, confiscation of property, and exile. Gradually families began to move over into Alsace, where there was more security, and by 1660 there were at least five congregations there, whose ministers in that year adopted the Dortrecht confession of faith as their standard. In 1659 the Canton of Berne decided to exterminate the Brethren in its territory, setting up a special Anabaptist Commission with special police for this purpose, and decreeing the exile of all Brethren. In 1671 and 1709 similar harsh decrees were passed, leading to the forcible deportation of hundreds down the Rhine on boats.

The chief place of refuge in the earlier years of this dreadful persecution was the principality called the Palatinate, just north of Alsace, located on both sides of the Rhine, with its capital at Heidelberg. Having suffered grievous devastation and loss of population through French invasions, this land was willing to do its utmost to improve its lot, and in 1664 invited Swiss Mennonites to settle under certain strict limitations. Only a limited number, not more than two hundred families, were to be allowed in the land at any one time, no meetinghouses were to be built or used, though worship in groups of not more than twenty persons might be held in homes, no baptisms could be performed, annual protection money must be paid, and no rights of citizenship could be granted. Even with these almost intolerable restrictions, the Palatinate was a paradise compared to the intolerable situation in Berne. The migration into the Palatinate was almost continuous for fifty years, with the largest contingent, over seven hundred souls, arriving in 1671. Some families found their way into such neighboring territories as Baden and Hesse, and by the beginning of the nineteenth century settlements were being made in Württemberg and Bavaria. Gradually the restrictions on the Mennonites were lifted in all these territories and well-established congregations were organized with a warm and active religious life.

Quite early (1695) the Bernese government had planned to ship some of its recalcitrant Mennonites to America, but this project miscarried. Ultimately, however, the Mennonites themselves decided to go to Pennsylvania, and beginning in 1707 a constantly growing stream of emigration, from both the Palatinate and Switzerland, carried thousands to the New World. The Mennonites of America who arrived before 1870, with few exceptions, had their origin in Switzerland, either directly, or indirectly via the Palatinate.

A bright aspect of this dark picture of persecution and emigration is the splendid relief work carried on by the Dutch Mennonites in behalf of their Swiss and Palatinate brethren. As early as 1660 they had interceded with the Bernese government on behalf of their persecuted coreligionists. They continued their intercession for many years, enlisting the aid of the Dutch government to this end. But more than this, they raised large funds to aid the destitute and needy, and to assist in financing emigration to Pennsylvania. This relief work was carried on for over one hundred years, largely through an excellent organization called "The Commission for Foreign Relief," founded in 1710.

The lot of the Mennonites in the Palatinate continued hard until the nineteenth century. In 1726 a law was passed, called the "Law of Retraction," permitting former owners of land held by Mennonites to repurchase such land at the original sale price at any time. In 1739 this right was limited to three years from date of sale, but it continued in force until 1801. Similar measures of oppression were invoked. Nevertheless, the Mennonites continued in their devoted, genuinely Christian way of life, greatly perplexing the authorities. An official statement by a government inspector in 1763 well represents the attitude of the Palatinate state toward the Mennonites at that time. "This sect is generally detested, and unquestionably should be exterminated. And yet daily experience indicates that better, more industrious, more efficient people cannot be found. Notwithstanding their heretical religion they should be taken as examples to be followed by people in general. One will never hear concerning them that they are guilty of any profanity, swearing, or of any misdeeds."

The spiritual condition of the Palatinate Mennonites continued good for a long time. A noteworthy conference at Ibersheim in 1803 gives clear indication of this. According to the decisions passed at this conference, young men who joined the army were to be excommunicated, mixed marriages were forbidden, ministers were to be selected by lot and serve without pay, drunkenness, swearing, gambling, dancing, and theater attendance were to be disciplined, vanity and pride, particularly in dress and everyday conduct, were to be discouraged, sisters must appear at the communion table with covered heads, church membership must be based on true conversion, applicants for baptism must be instructed, and children below fourteen could not be accepted as members. In the nineteenth century gradually many of these requirements were relaxed, particularly by the introduction of a salaried ministry and the abandonment of nonresist-

61

ance, but a strong and active life prevailed until the last generation. The industry and intelligence of these people in their chosen occupation of farming was renowned far and wide, and one of their number, David Möllinger (1709-86), is credited with the introduction of the crop rotation system, one of the greatest advances in modern scientific agriculture.

Meanwhile the lot of the Brethren in the old homeland in Switzerland continued to be almost unbearably hard. As late as 1753 Bernese Mennonites were sold to the French and Venetian navies as galley slaves on the Mediterranean, and Mennonite children were legally disinherited. Marriages and burials by Mennonite ministers were forbidden. As late as 1811 twenty-seven Mennonite children in Langnau, Switzerland, were forcibly baptized in the state church, and repeatedly Mennonite children were forcibly taken to catechism by the police. But finally in 1815 full toleration was granted, with exemption from military service on payment of a substitute fee.

In spite of this persecution, a serious schism arose among the Swiss and Alsatian churches. This was the Amish schism of 1693-97, which has been described in another section. In 1832-35 another smaller division occurred, this time limited to a group of sixty members of the Emmenthal church. From this division developed what was first called "Die Neu-Täufer," in America "New Amish," but later named "The Christian Apostolic Church." First immigrants to America from this group came to New York, Ohio, and Illinois in 1846 and after. Their largest settlement is around Morton, Illinois.

Emigration from the Swiss Mennonite churches and the Alsatian Amish churches began again on a large scale after the Napoleonic wars in Europe, and the Revolutionary War and the War of 1812 in America, were past. From 1817 to the American Civil War, large settlements were made in the United States and Canada by emigrants from these regions.

One unfortunate effect of the centuries of persecution upon Swiss and South German Mennonites was the creation of a quietistic spirit. The passive attitude toward the world, and even toward aggressive action within their own groups, created a spirit of resignation and self-depreciation which amounted to a strong inferiority feeling which inhibited action. The sense of witness was largely lost, even to their own children. For instance, the descendants of the not more than one thousand exiles who left Switzerland for the Palatinate between 1671 and 1711, many of whom came to America, today number probably more than 50,000, while the descendants of those who remained behind in Switzerland today number less than 2,000.* In fact, the Mennonite population of Switzerland and South Germany has remained almost static for a hundred years, in some places has even declined. Prior to World War II these groups were being increasingly assimilated to the surrounding culture, so that the sense of uniqueness and mission which so strongly characterized the first Swiss Brethren was rapidly being lost. Since the war, however, these churches have experienced a new vitality, so that their present state is more encouraging.

b. Dutch Mennonites in North Germany and Their Experiences to 1914

The original Dutch Mennonite movement founded by the Philips brothers and Menno Simons, 1533-36, was carried by zealous evangelists and faithful elders throughout a large extent of territory along the North Sea coast and Southern Baltic area from Antwerp to Danzig, and inland to Aix-la-Chapelle, Cologne, and the Ruhr. The strongest centers of the movement were in the provinces of North and South Holland and Friesland, together with Antwerp, Emden, Holstein, and the Vistula delta. Severe persecution, however, early wiped out the movement in Flanders and Holstein, as well as in the Cologne and Ruhr areas. Later refugees from Holland and Friesland revived some of these congregations and established new ones. This was particularly true after 1600, when large congregations were developed in Crefeld (after 1620), in Hamburg-Altona, and in the Vistula delta around Danzig. The congregations in Crefeld, Hamburg, and Danzig were composed of artisans and merchants, while those in the Vistula delta were composed of farmers who did remarkable work in draining and developing the swamp lands of the Vistula delta. In the Netherlands also many congregations were established in the cities, where they were composed of artisans and merchants largely of the middle classes, although peasant congregations were also established, particularly in Friesland. Amsterdam, Rotterdam, Haarlem, The Hague, Groningen, Deventer, Utrecht, Leeuwarden—all became seats of large congregations which have remained so to the present day, some numbering into the thousands of members, with Amsterdam having over seven thousand.

* Another 3,000 and more are in America today, representing a nineteenth-century immigration.

The urban and merchant character of Dutch-North German Mennonitism made for the development of a different type from the peasant farming type in Mennonitism in Switzerland and South Germany. With growing toleration in the Netherlands, Mennonites grew wealthy and influential, partook increasingly of the culture of their country, and became more and more a part of upper middle class Dutch life. At first, particularly in the seventeenth century, this was all to the good. The churches prospered, were aggressive, and enjoyed an active and sound religious life. But in the eighteenth century an inevitable decline set in. Wealth and the desire for social recognition weakened the sturdy faith of the martyr forefathers. Mennonites not only began to be more in the world round about them, but began to be more like it. And when they were more like it, it was easy to move across the border line into the world. Even the statistics of membership tell the tragic story of a movement that almost died after persecution was past, though persecution had never been able to crush it. It is said that the entire Mennonite population of Holland declined from 160,000 souls in 1700 to about 30,000 souls in 1820. Over one hundred congregations died out completely, while others suffered drastic losses. In the ninteenth century there was again a gradual increase, until at the present time the population numbers about 70,000.

The inner life of the Mennonites of Holland during this period also had its ups and downs. In the latter half of the sixteenth century serious divisions arose which broke up the entire body into three major groups, the Flemish, the Frisians, and the Waterlanders, with additional smaller divisions on the side. These divisions spread throughout the churches of North Germany and into the Danzig region. They were carried over into Russia by the immigrants from Danzig in 1789-1810, and were not overcome in that country until after the emigration of 1874. In Holland fortunately they were overcome by reunions and confederations long before that time. Since 1800 the Dutch Mennonites have been to all practical purposes a united body, organized into a conference called "The General Mennonite Society." In 1847 the first Mennonite foreign mission was established in Java by Dutch Mennonites.

Scarcely was the period of division of the late sixteenth century past, when a liberal theological movement known as Socinianism found its way into the churches in the early seventeenth century, doing considerable damage. This movement was unitarian in its theology.

In the latter part of the century a pietistic revival exerted a wholesome influence for a long time, but it weakened the unique character of Mennonitism and made it more like the conventional, orthodox Protestant churches of the time. Theological liberalism came into the churches again in the nineteenth century, this time in the form of rationalistic modernism, and succeeded in doing what Socinianism failed to accomplish, namely, to transform Dutch Mennonitism into a unitarian body. In the early part of the twentieth century also such typical Mennonite principles as nonresistance were completely abandoned. Thus Dutch Mennonitism at the beginning of World War I was scarcely recognizable in terms of the historic faith of its founders; indeed it consciously repudiated Menno to a large extent. The city churches of Northwest Germany, such as Emden and Crefeld, largely followed the Dutch churches in this modernistic trend.

At this point came new stirrings, however, to the reawakening of an interest and a concern for historic Dutch Mennonitism. The *Gemeentedagbeweging,* established in 1920, partly under English Quaker influence, marked the beginning of the restoration of a more evangelical theology, coupled with more aggressive activity and a revival of interest in historic Mennonite principles, such as nonresistance. This development has continued at an even greater pace since World War II, so that by the mid-twentieth century the Dutch Mennonite Church was an extremely vital factor within world Mennonitism.

Dutch Mennonitism has made large contributions to American Mennonitism. Dutch Mennonite literature, particularly in the writings of Menno Simons, Dirk Philips, J. P. Schabalie *(The Wandering Soul),* T. J. van Braght *(The Martyrs' Mirror),* has been more influential in America than any other Mennonite literature, for the Swiss and Russian Mennonites had practically no literature of their own. Furthermore, all of the confessions of faith of the various American groups are either Dutch confessions or are based on them. For instance, the Dortrecht Confession of 1632 is the official confession of the (old) Mennonites, the Amish, and all groups related to them, numbering perhaps 115,000 or more baptized members, and the General Conference Mennonite Church uses the Cornelis Ris Confession of 1747.

The churches of eastern Germany around Danzig and in the Vistula delta retained their ancient faith and Mennonite principles sturdily until the last half century. They continued to keep a strong orthodox and evangelical theology, and preserved such Mennonite principles as simplicity and nonswearing, much like the South Germans. But after the militarization of Prussia in the nineteenth century and the abolition of exemption from military service in 1868, they gradually abandoned nonresistance, though remnants of the principle were retained by ever smaller fractions up to World War I.

CHAPTER 11

The Migration to Russia

Mennonites have made many migrations for conscience' sake, but (until 1923) none in such a large and compact settlement as that from Eastern Prussia to Russia one hundred and fifty years ago. The occasion for this migration was the generous offer of the Russian government to induce settlers to occupy the territory in the Ukraine then recently conquered from Turkey, but the cause was the persecution of the Mennonites of Prussia by the Prussian authorities. Both the Prussian state and the Lutheran state church were determined to prevent any further growth of Mennonitism in the land, for they had seen the Mennonites become increasingly prosperous and numerous during the eighteenth century. Furthermore the nonresistant Mennonites were a threat to the military power of the growing Prussian state, which was taking the lead in militaristic policies among the states of Europe. Many restrictive measures were imposed. Mennonites were forbidden to increase their landholdings except by special permission. They were forced to pay special taxes in lieu of military service, as well as to pay taxes for the support of the Lutheran Church.

Small wonder that the Mennonites were ready to consider the generous offer which the Russian government made them through a special envoy in 1786, which was confirmed by delegates sent on a tour of inspection to Russia the same year. This offer included the following remarkable terms: free transportation to Russia; one hundred and seventy-five acres of free land per family; a loan of $250.00 and support for each family at a cheap rate until the first harvest; complete religious freedom; complete freedom of language and schools; complete military exemption; self-government within their settlements; no taxes for ten years and only a nominal federal tax thereafter. Only one limitation was made, namely, that the Mennonites do no religious work among the native Russians. These privileges were guaranteed in a special imperial decree in perpetuity, i.e., "forever."

The first group of two hundred and twenty-eight families left the region of Danzig in the fall of 1788 and traveled overland by wagon reaching their new home on the Chortitza creek in the summer of 1789. Further settlers followed, and by 1800 the settlement on the Chortitza, called later the "Old Colony," numbered over four hundred families, with a population of probably two thousand souls. The Chortitza settlement lies on the River Dnieper, near the great dam and power plant of Dnieperstroi.

A second large settlement was founded in 1803 along the Molotschna River, some sixty miles south of the Chortitza settlement, with the arrival of three hundred and forty-two families from Prussia. Six years later ninety-nine more families came to the Molotschna, and in 1820 two hundred and fifteen more. By 1840 a total of seven hundred and fifty families had arrived on the Molotschna, which now was larger than the "Old Colony." A total of 1,150 families with probably not less than 6,000 souls thus found their way from Prussia to South Russia in the fifty years from 1789 to 1840, most of whom settled in two large compact groups. Other smaller groups found their way to South Russia later.

The new settlements in Russia, called colonies, made remarkable progress in every way during more than a century following their establishment, up to the outbreak of World War I in 1914. In spite of the large emigration of 1874-80, which drained away to America at least one third of the population, the total Mennonite population in Russia in 1914 is estimated to have grown to 100,000 souls, all through natural family increase. The land in the original two colonies was limited; hence the population growth had to be accommodated in so-called "daughter colonies." These new colonies were largely frontier areas purchased by the mother colonies, and sold on easier terms to young families in need of land. The first of these new colonies was founded in 1836, the last just before World War I, although as late as 1927 a colony was established along the Amur River on the Russian-Manchurian border. The largest of these daughter colonies was established by the Choritza colony in 1907-10 in Western Siberia, where two hundred families were settled at one time. Other settlements were made in the Crimea, the Caucasus, the Middle Volga, Orenburg, Ufa, and many places in between. It must be said that at first the original colonies were inclined to be selfish with their wealth and did not provide for the new families until practically forced to do so by serious unrest after more than half of the population had become "landless."

The religious history of the Russian settlements is of great interest, though space will not permit extended discussion. The advantages and dangers of closed colony life in a foreign culture are well illustrated by this history. The settlements were handicapped by the fact that certain divisions had been brought with them from Prussia which took long to overcome. But more serious was the fact that gradually membership in the church came to be regarded as a matter of course, actually a matter of birth, and was no longer based on a personal experience of conversion. The lack of stimulation from the outside, and the hardships of pioneer life, brought about a gradual spiritual decline. Strict discipline was maintained for deviations from church regulations, but often external compulsions took the place of inner sanctification, and gradually morals declined in many respects, so that discipline was very uneven. Ministers seldom preached or exercised a pastoral ministry, the custom being to read sermons and to follow the traditions of the past. Since local government was in the hands of the settlements, Mennonites found themselves in the position of exercising the police power and operating on a basis of external compulsion, again to the detriment of spiritual life. The lack of opportunity for evangelism and missionary work (forbidden at the very beginning by the government) also contributed to cutting the nerve of the impulse to witness, and turned Mennonite energies in the direction of building up a "Mennonite culture." These were some of the disadvantages of the closed colony life.

Nevertheless criticism must not be too severe. In spite of weaknesses and failures, the Mennonites throughout Russia almost to a man remained staunch defenders of the historic Mennonite principles of nonresistance, nonswearing of oaths, the simple life, nonconformity to the world, and the demand for consistent living, even though they did not always maintain a perfect practice of these doctrines. They likewise maintained the orthodox Christian faith, based their doctrines and practices on the Bible, and gave the church a central and powerful place in their life.

As elsewhere, the Mennonites in Russia also suffered from schisms. Besides the small division which occurred in the years 1812-19 in the Molotschna colony, which led to the formation of the much stricter "Kleine Gemeinde" under Preacher Klaas Reimer, one major division occurred in Russian Mennonitism which was to have great significance. It was the organization of the Mennonite Brethren Church at Gnadenfeld in the Molotschna colony in 1860. Later a group of the Kleine Gemeinde living in the Crimea separated from that body, and called themselves the Krimmer (Crimean) Mennonite Brethren Church. These three separated groups, in addition to the main body of Russian Mennonites, making a total of four bodies, were all represented in the migration to America in 1874-80. It must not be thought of course that the main body of Mennonite congregations in Russia constituted a well-organized unit, for this was not the case.

The division of 1860 is of great interest because it was caused by and led to a genuine revival and reform of the somewhat impoverished religious life of the Russian Mennonites. The revival came from outside influence in the person of Edward Wüst, able preacher and evangelist of a Lutheran pietist settlement near the Molotschna colony. In spite of some extremes, which it must be admitted were repeated at first by his Mennonite disciples, Wüst's influence did great good among the Mennonites. He stressed the importance of a personal Christian experience, of continuing prayer and spiritual fellowship with God, and of a devoted Christian life. His weakness was to stress emotion at the expense of practical Christian holiness. Those Mennonites in the Molotschna who experienced a spiritual awakening through Wüst's preaching naturally became acutely conscious of the deficiencies among the rather tradition-bound Mennonite churches of which they had until then been a part. They saw too the need for a stricter discipline. At once they went into action, but their demands for reform met with little or no response from the leaders of the church. Indeed they aroused bitter opposition. Believing that they could not tolerate the old church longer, eighteen members withdrew from the church at Gnadenfeld, and organized a brotherhood which would propagate their views. It is astonishing to us today to note that the authorities of the old church actually persecuted the new body, causing arrests and punishment, and threatening them with loss of civil rights.

It must not be forgotten that a religious awakening was already in progress in the Mennonite churches of Russia at this time, and that the formation of the Mennonite Brethren Church undoubtedly hastened the progress of this revival. The division had the beneficial effect of awakening intelligent leaders in the old church to the need of genuine reform. Henceforth there was general progress toward better things religiously throughout Russian Mennonitism.

Space will not permit extensive description of the remarkable cultural and economic development of the Russian Mennonite settlements during their long history in South Russia. The new homeland gave Mennonites for the first time in history an opportunity not only to develop their religious life according to their conscience, but also to develop their economic life and cultural genius with complete freedom. Unlimited expansion was possible in every direction. At first the Mennonites were handicapped by the traditions of their Prussian delta land origins, but gradually with foresighted leaders new methods of farming were developed, new crops were introduced, and new cooperative organizations were established. The great leader in this movement was a man named Johann Cornies, president from 1830 to 1848 of an agricultural society, a great organizer and agricultural expert. By the time of World War I the Mennonites had a high per capita wealth, based largely on very productive land and advanced methods of farming, but based also on milling and manufacturing enterprises. Among other things they manufactured most of the agricultural implements produced in Russia.

Just as significant as the economic progress of the colonies was their progress in educational and cultural work. They supported their own schools, including high schools and normal schools. They established hospitals and asylums, and operated efficient mutual aid insurance organizations. All this the World War and the ensuing Bolshevist Revolution brought to a sudden end.

The greatest crisis in Russian Mennonitism came with the loss of special privileges, particularly of military exemption in 1870, due to the growing militarization of Russia and the policy of russifying foreign elements such as the German colonies. When all attempts of the Mennonites to retain their privileges failed, large numbers decided to emigrate. In 1873 twelve delegates were sent to the United States and Canada to determine the advisability of settlement in America, and to select the best locations for settlement. They were also to attempt to secure guarantees of religious liberty and military exemption. The outcome of this trip of inspection was highly favorable, and resulted in the migration of at least 18,000 Russian Mennonites to America in the years 1874-80, of whom over 6,000 arrived in the first year, 1874. About one third went to Manitoba, the rest largely to Kansas, with settlements in Nebraska, South Dakota, and Minnesota.

Today the descendants of these settlers, including ten thousand in Mexico and two thousand in Paraguay, number well over 100,000 souls.

Meanwhile the Russian government, in fear of losing the entire Mennonite population, who were among its most desirable citizens, modified its demands on the Mennonites. Once more military exemption was promised, provided the Mennonites would give state service outside the army, such as forestry service. A plan of state forestry service, largely at church expense, was finally adopted and put into effect in 1880, to the general satisfaction of the Mennonites who stayed in Russia as well as of their government. Thus the principle of nonresistance was maintained. From the point of view of American Mennonitism the whole crisis was beneficial because it brought a large infusion of new elements. In view of the tragic fate of the Mennonites under the Bolshevist regime after 1917, the emigration to America in 1874 proved to be providential. From this new base in America the descendants of Russian Mennonitism joined with the older American Mennonite groups in the first united relief effort by American Mennonites through the newly organized Mennonite Central Committee, saving many thousands of the brethren in their old homeland from death during the famine of 1920-22, and helping some 25,000 to new homes in Canada, the United States, and South America.

CHAPTER 12

European Mennonites
During the World Wars

In a certain sense the World War of 1914-18, calamitous though it was, should not mark a new period in European Mennonitism. Yet, in the increasing perspective of change since that time, it is becoming clear that this is truly the case.

It is most striking in the case of the Mennonites of Russia. The account of what has happened in Russia is a harrowing story. The collapse of the old Russian Czarist regime and the establishment of atheistic communism in the form of the Bolshevist regime now known as the Soviet state wrought a tragedy as great as any experienced in all Mennonite history, the only possible exception being the persecutions of the sixteenth century.

At first the need for cautious evolution, and the handicaps of civil war and famine, made for a slow application of collectivization and anti-Christianity. But finally the full revolution came to the Mennonite colonies. Especially after 1930 Mennonite communities were broken up, worship was suppressed, church life was destroyed, and Mennonite youths by the thousands were communized. The old colonies with their high culture, wealth, and civil life were largely wiped out. Those Mennonites who remained again became "The Quiet in the Land," in some cases exiled or resettled, perhaps long kept in concentration camps, refraining from outward expression and organization, and subject to the educational processes of the anti-Christian communist state which seeks to mold their children's life and faith after the pattern of Bolshevist paganism.

Concurrent with this destruction of Mennonite *life* came the destruction of Mennonite *lives* by the thousands. The great famine of 1920-22 did not result in a heavy loss of life because of the splendid relief work carried on by the American Mennonites at this time. But the "liquidation" of the "Kulak," or prosperous peasant class, by the government in 1927-32, followed by the severe famine of 1933-34, did.

We should not overlook the thrilling rescue of over 25,000 Mennonites from Russia in the two great migrations of 1923-30. In the first migration 20,000 were brought to Canada under the direction of the Canadian Mennonite Board of Colonization. In the latter migration, in which the Mennonite Central Committee played the larger role, another 5,000 were brought to Canada, Brazil, and Paraguay.

In Russia the execution, deportation to the forests of Vologda and Archangel, to the gold mines of the Urals, or to Siberia, or merely "resettlement" in other places begun in 1929, continued until 1940. Hardly any of the exiled persons (mostly men) ever returned and most of them have, no doubt, meanwhile perished. This wave of exile swept not only the Chortitza and other Mennonite settlements, but also the Russian population in general.

Immediately after the beginning of the invasion of the Ukraine by the German army in 1941 the Soviet government organized an evacuation of all population of German background beyond the Ural Mountains. That fall the Neu-Samara Mennonite settlement on the Volga was entirely evacuated. Most of the Mennonite settlements east of the Dnieper River, including such large settlements as the Molotschna, Memrik, and others, were almost totally evacuated to Siberia. From the Chortitza settlement, located west of the Dnieper River, only about 1,300 out of the 14,000 inhabitants were evacuated because the German army moved in so swiftly. This explains why most of the Mennonites who have been moved to North and South America after World War II are from the Chortitza settlement.

During the short German occupation the Mennonites more or less resumed their former way of life. Then in the fall of 1943 after the defeat of the German army another evacuation took place. This time it was westward. The women that were left in the Molotschna settlement drove horses and wagons with what was left of their family and possessions toward the Polish border and Prussia, from where their forefathers had come nearly 150 years before. About 12,000 Mennonites from the Chortitza settlement were taken to Germany by train. Most of these evacuees were to be settled in the region called Warthegau (former Posen) and other places. The so-called Galician Mennonites from Poland were also among them. These plans were of short duration. In January, 1945, when the Red army entered Germany proper, a general mass movement of refugees farther westward started.

The Prussian Mennonites of the Vistula delta joined the masses fleeing westward. In March, 1945, when Danzig was captured, part of the population fled westward and about 200,000 were taken by ship to German-occupied cities in Denmark. Among them were 4,000 Mennonites who lived behind barbed wire until 1948, when most of them were taken to West Germany. The estimated number of Mennonites reaching Germany from Russia in 1941-43 is 35,000. When the remnants had been gathered into displaced persons' camps in 1945-47 the total was about 12,000. Thus if the above estimate is correct, more than 20,000 perished or were forcibly repatriated, not to their homes in the Ukraine but beyond the Ural Mountains to slave labor camps. It must be remembered also that not all Mennonites were in camps.

Almost insurmountable obstacles had to be overcome before emigration was possible, but with the co-operation of the MCC refugee staff, the International Refugee Organization, and the American and British occupational authorities a great many Russian Mennonites were able to leave Germany for new homes in North and South America. Canada received nearly 8,000; Paraguay, nearly 5,000; and the United States, 400. About 1,000 Danzig and Prussian Mennonites migrated to Uruguay and about 300 to Canada.

The second major effect of World War I which has influenced the course of history for European Mennonitism was the rise of National Socialism and the Hitler regime in Germany. The German defeat in World War I had a sobering effect on the Mennonites of Germany, and their increased contact with the Russian and American Mennonites through relief work had brought new influences to bear upon them which contributed to a revived interest in nonresistance in some quarters. The coming of Hitler's movement in 1923, however, with its rise to full control of the German state in 1933, and the reintroduction of militarism under totalitarianism, nipped this movement in the bud. Strangely enough National Socialism found many adherents among the German Mennonites, primarily in Eastern Prussia, and the resistance of the older and more conservative leaders to the new trend was unable to stem the tide. A striking expression of the new spirit was the formal renunciation of nonresistance by the first session of the newly organized German Mennonite Conference of 1935.

Following World War II, however, with an even greater American relief work than after the first war, and with an expanded and intensified international Mennonite experience, the earlier revival which had been thwarted was renewed once more until today the German Mennonites have a closer working relationship with their brethren in other European countries and in North America than ever before in their history. Interest in historic Mennonitism is much alive today. The German government once more gives recognition to conscientious objectors and a number of young German Mennonites are doing alternative service as "CO's."

Mennonitism in Holland had shown many signs of new life after World War I. Through the *Gemeentedagbeweging*, briefly described in the preceding chapter, there came a revival of a warmer, more evangelical religious life in certain quarters, and a growing interest in the faith of the forefathers, particularly in the principle of nonresistance. Coupled with this was increased activity, support of missions, and a growing social conscience. The war interfered with this evolution, particularly after the occupation of Holland in 1940, but the pressure of the events of war and the occupation by the Germans increased rather than decreased the forces making for spiritual revival. Postwar developments have brought further progress among the Dutch Mennonites.

An interesting phase of recent history in Europe has been the growing interest in international Mennonite contacts. This found expression in seven "world conferences" of Mennonites, in 1925, 1930, 1936, 1948, 1952, 1957, and 1962. The occasion of the first was the four hundredth anniversary of the founding of the Mennonite Church; it was held in Basel, Switzerland. The second was a "relief conference," related to the relief ministry for the Russian Mennonites, and was held in Danzig. The occasion of the third was the four hundredth anniversary of Menno Simons' conversion, and was held at Amsterdam in 1936. All three of these earlier conferences were limited largely to unofficial participation of German and Dutch Mennonites, with a few delegates from Switzerland and North America. The 1948 conference in Goshen, Indiana, and North Newton, Kansas, was largely North American, with small delegations from Europe and South America. The 1952 and 1957 conferences at Basel, Switzerland, and Karlsruhe, Germany, were largely attended from both North America and Europe and were landmarks in world Mennonite co-operation. Most largely attended of all, however, was the seventh Mennonite World Conference held at Kitchener, Ontario, in 1962, with an official registration of 12,207 persons. Thousands of others who did not register attended one or more sessions and it is estimated that a total of 25,000 participated in the conference at some point. The registration list shows 141 official delegates from Germany, 110 from the Netherlands, 37 from France, 33 from Switzerland, 12 from South America, four from India, two each from England, Indonesia, and Japan; and one each from Africa and Taiwan. This was truly an international conference, and very likely the largest single gathering of Mennonites at any one time throughout 437 years of history.

In the larger perspective it is clear that the center of gravity of world Mennonitism is now in North America. This is the case not merely because of America's much larger Mennonite population—nearly 250,000 baptized members out of a total world membership of 430,000, including the younger churches of Africa and Asia—nor because of the more effective organization of activities, but primarily because the vigor and power of Mennonitism in America is still unimpaired, and most of all because it has kept a strong evangelical faith and with it the essence of the historic Mennonite heritage. Mennonites of America now stand in the breach. Theirs is the opportunity to lead a world-wide revival of these great principles and to rally all Mennonites everywhere in a forward movement. In this mission they are being actively supported by a growing number of European Mennonites.

PART II

MENNONITES IN AMERICA

BY C. HENRY SMITH

D. How and Where Mennonites Settled in America

CHAPTER 13

Early Settlements

The early Mennonites in America, like the Puritans of New England, were a select people, selected on the basis of a tender conscience against war and religious intolerance. At the time they began their migration to America, in 1683, the state churches in Europe were still closely enough associated with the state governments to make life miserable for all those who did not share the religious beliefs of their persecutors. To be sure, the day of burning men and women at the stake was past, but nonconformists were still greatly limited in their religious rights.

Crefeld, the chief city of the independent county of Moers, was the original home of the first Mennonite immigrants to Pennsylvania, and at the time the most tolerant of all the cities of this area. Even here both the Quakers and the Mennonites, and especially the former, were still subjected to most humiliating and oppressive religious and civil restrictions. In the Palatinate in southwestern Germany, the European homeland of nearly all the Mennonites of Lancaster and Franconia in Pennsylvania, they suffered all sorts of restrictions upon their religious and civil liberties. Throughout the entire eighteenth century the Palatine counts imposed on them special taxes in the form of protection money for the mere privilege of remaining in the land. Mennonites were denied the privilege of living in the cities and learning a trade; they were forbidden to make converts among the members of the state churches; they were forced to sell their lands to members of the state church upon the request of the latter, without any remuneration above the original cost for any improvements they may have made on their properties in the meantime; and finally, they were denied the right of burial in the public cemeteries. In fact, Mennonites were classed with the Jews as a merely tolerated people, with no inherent rights, either civil or religious, except such as the ruling authorities were willing to grant them from time to time. It was these religious and civil restrictions, together with the economic distress caused largely by the numerous wars fought on Palatine soil by the nations of central Europe throughout the entire century, that were responsible for the continuous stream of Mennonite emigration to the "Paradise of Pennsylvania" during this period.

New York and Delaware

The first Mennonites to touch American soil, so far as we have any records, were a few stray Dutch merchants and colonists who followed their fellow countrymen from Holland to their possessions in the New World when New York was still New Amsterdam. Beyond a few references, however, in the colonial documents, here and there, beginning as early as 1643, there is no record anywhere of an enduring settlement or an organized congregation.

A little later, in 1663, Cornelisz Pieter Plockhoy, a Dutch dreamer of social utopias, and perhaps a member of the liberal Socinian wing of the Dutch Mennonites, planted a colony of twenty-five Mennonite families along the southern coast of what is now the state of Delaware. But of this colony, too, no record is left except that in 1664, during the Dutch-English war, this settlement was destroyed "to a very naile" by an English marauding party, and Plockhoy together with his wife sometime later appeared penniless at the Germantown colony, where his few wants were cared for during the rest of his days.

Pennsylvania

GERMANTOWN. The first permanent Mennonite settlement on this side of the Atlantic was founded in 1683 in what is now Germantown, a part of the present Philadelphia, by a group of thirteen families from the city of Crefeld and surrounding territory along the lower German Rhine. Most of these original families were of Dutch extraction, though at the time they came Crefeld was German territory. For some time before this, Quaker missionaries from England, including George Fox and William Penn themselves, had frequently visited western Germany with the result that a number of small Quaker groups had been established among the Mennonites of these regions. The Quakers, because of their aggressive missionary zeal, were more harshly treated by the German ruling authorities than were the milder Mennonites, and so were especially susceptible to Penn's invitation to join his "holy experiment" in the New World. In fact, among the thirteen original families composing the Germantown colony, twelve (although originally Mennonites) were soon affiliated with the Quakers. Only one, Jan Lensen, remained a Mennonite.

This single bona fide Mennonite no doubt at first worshiped with the Quakers, as did also Pastorius, a former Lutheran pietist who was the land agent for the Frankfort Land Company, and from whom the first settlers bought all their farming lots. In a few years, however, sufficient new Mennonite arrivals justified the founding of a separate Mennonite congregation. In 1690, William Rittenhouse, ancestor of a long line of distinguished families, was elected the first Mennonite minister in America. In 1708 the first Mennonite log cabin meetinghouse was erected, to be succeeded in 1770 by the little stone building still standing and used for worship.

The Germantown congregation never grew large. Later immigrants passed it by for the cheaper lands farther west along the Skippack and the Conestoga. By 1712 the combined membership of the Germantown and the Skippack churches was ninety-nine. The congregation finally became extinct, to be revived, however, in 1864 under the pastorate of F. R. S. Hunsicker. It remains today a small group of some thirty members, affiliated with the General Conference branch of the denomination.

SKIPPACK—FRANCONIA. The colony along the Skippack Creek, a daughter colony of Germantown, was founded in 1702 by Matthias van Bebber, who bought a large tract of land in this area. Soon other Mennonites from Germantown and directly from the Palatinate located here, in course of time forming almost a solid Mennonite community along the Skippack and the Perkiomen, with some scattered settlements in nearby regions. This community today has a total population, including children, of some twelve thousand souls. The largest single group in the settlement is known as the Franconia Conference of the (old) Mennonites.

LANCASTER COUNTY. By far the largest Mennonite settlement of the colonial period was that made along the Conestoga in 1710 and the years following by immigrants directly from the Palatinate.

83

The chief causes of this migration were religious oppression, the economic poverty prevailing throughout the Palatinate due to the continual French-German wars that had almost completely devastated this region, and the liberal promises of William Penn. The names appearing on the land warrant issued in 1710 to the pioneer settlers here were John Rudolph Bundely, Martin Kendig, Jacob Miller, Hans Graff, Hans Herr, Christian Herr, Martin Oberholts, Hans Funk, Michael Oberholts, and Weyndel Bowman, "Switzers, lately arrived in the Province." These were among the Swiss refugees and their descendants who had been exiled from the Canton of Berne in 1671 and the following years and had located in the Palatinate because of persecution in Switzerland.

Being well pleased with the rich limestone soil along the Conestoga, and the religious liberty granted them by William Penn, the pioneers sent a messenger back to their homeland, urging their fellow sufferers to join them. Many of the Palatines accepted this invitation. In the years that followed, up to the French and Indian War in 1754, every year saw groups of new immigrants arriving, who bought land among the first settlers. The colony grew until rural Lancaster became almost solidly Mennonite.

Today Lancaster city is the center of the largest compact Mennonite and Amish community in North America, and since the dissolution of the Mennonite settlements in Russia, probably of the world, with a total of over 25,000 baptized members living within a radius of 25 miles, in over 150 congregations.

THE AMISH. The members of the Amish branch of the church did not have much religious affiliation with the Mennonites, either in the Palatinate or in Pennsylvania, during this period. While there may have been an occasional Amish immigrant among the first Mennonite settlements, it was not until the arrival of Jacob Hochstetler in 1736, and a group of other Amishmen, that a separate congregation was organized in what is now Berks County, near a gap in the Blue Mountains, along Northkill Creek.

This choice of a location near the Indian frontier turned out to be a mistake; for in 1757, during the Indian wars, the Indians invaded the colony, and after killing several members of the Hochstetler family, drove the rest of the colonists back to the older settlements. This practically annihilated the Northkill colony. The scattered members later formed settlements in southern Berks and eastern Lancaster, which later spread over into Chester County. The total number of

Amish arrivals during the period before the Revolution was not large, perhaps not much beyond five hundred.

There was probably little difference at this time between the Amish and Mennonites in either social practice or outward form. Both still wore beards, and hooks and eyes, as did their forebears in the Palatinate and Switzerland. The chief difference was in the insistence by the Amish on the practice of avoidance.

The total number of Amish and Mennonite immigrants to Pennsylvania in the eighteenth century was perhaps not much above three thousand souls, but their descendants today, still of the Mennonite faith, not counting those who left the church of their fathers, have grown to approximately two hundred thousand, gathered together in compact groups of varying sizes throughout all the northern states almost in a beeline straight west of the original Pennsylvania home, as far as Colorado, Idaho, and Oregon, and including Ontario, Canada.

CHAPTER 14

Expansion of Pennsylvania Settlements Before 1800

Long before the middle of the eighteenth century, the choice lands of the southeastern tip of Pennsylvania had been taken over by the Quakers, Germans, and Scotch Irish. The second generation of the pioneer settlers consequently had to search for homes farther out on the expanding frontier. The surplus Mennonite population joined in this search, spreading new colonies over into the nearby counties of Lebanon, York, Lehigh, and down the Cumberland Valley through Maryland into the fertile Shenandoah Valley of Virginia.

Virginia

Before 1730 the Mennonites had joined other Lancaster County Germans in founding one of the first German settlements in Virginia, in what is now Page County, to be followed later by another small group in Shenandoah County. These small Mennonite colonies did not last long. But before 1800, these, together with others from Pennsylvania, had established a substantial community farther up the Shenandoah, in Linville Valley north of Harrisonburg, in what is now Rockingham County. Singers Glen, a little village at the head of this valley, finally became the literary and musical center of this whole region, covering a rather wide area. Here Joseph Funk, from a long line of literary Funks, in the early part of the nineteenth century established a printing press on which he published Mennonite religious tracts and books, as well as musical productions, including the well-known *Harmonia Sacra,* which went through numerous editions in the years that followed and, like the McGuffey readers in Ohio, is still the source of much musical pleasure on special occasions to the old-timers.

The Virginians were the only Mennonites to live in pro-slavery territory before the Civil War. To their credit be it said that while slavery was practiced by their non-Mennonite neighbors all about them, Mennonites themselves never held slaves, nor sanctioned the institution. As late as 1864, right in the middle of the war, when it took courage to take the stand, they went on record in a church conference resolution to the following effect:

> Decided that inasmuch as it is against our creed and discipline to own or traffic in slaves, so it is also forbidden a brother to hire slaves unless such slaves be entitled to receive the pay for such labor by the consent of the owner. But where neighbors exchange labor, the labor of slaves may be received.

The baptized Mennonite membership of Virginia today numbers approximately five thousand, and is almost entirely of the (old) Mennonite branch of the church.

Western Pennsylvania

In the meantime small groups of both Mennonites and Amish were finding their way to the frontiers of western Pennsylvania. As early as 1765, a small band of pioneers, following the winding course of the Juniata into the interior of the province, located a small congregation in what is now Snyder County, to be followed, later, by others into Somerset, Fayette, and Westmoreland counties. Johnstown, the city made famous by the flood of the eighties of the past century, received its name from an Amishman who owned the land on which the town was first built. The Scottdale Mennonite community was founded about 1790. The largest community of this period was that established by the Amish near the close of the century in the beautiful Kishacoquillas Valley, in what is now Mifflin County. This settlement in course of time spread out over the whole southern half of the valley, with Belleville as its chief center. From here and Somerset County came also, in the next century, the settlers of many of the Amish communities to be established in states farther west, such as Ohio, Indiana, and Missouri.

Ontario

Soon after the Revolutionary War, during the period of economic anarchy and political uncertainty that followed the war, numerous Pennsylvania Loyalists, who still preferred the familiar though foreign Union Jack to their own new Stars and Stripes, largely because they were opposed to "rebellion" against established government, started out for the primitive forests of Upper Canada, just across the Niagara, preferring also the cheap uncultivated lands across the border to the high priced farms of their own communities. The Canadian government, too, very anxious for industrious and peaceful farmers to settle its own frontier lands, offered special inducements to prospective land seekers. Much of Upper Canada was settled by American Loyalists.

Among the early, if not the earliest, immigrants to trek to the lands across the Falls were several Mennonite groups from Bucks and Franklin counties, who made their first appearance across the border as early as 1786. About the turn of the century several substantial communities of Mennonites were established in what is now Welland, Lincoln, and Waterloo counties, followed later by other small groups in other nearby regions, especially in York County, near Toronto. The most important and the largest of these colonies was the one in Waterloo County. Here along the Grand River the Mennonites were among the very first of white settlers to locate on virgin soil. The region round about was still a primitive wilderness. In course of time a small thriving village was established, which they finally called Berlin, a name which during World War I was changed to Kitchener.

This exodus of the Mennonites to the north, of course, like all movements to a new home, was the result of a number of causes— economic pressure, high price of land in the home community, political uncertainty for the future at first, the cheap lands of Ontario together with liberal terms offered by the Ontario government, and also, no doubt, not least, the fact that the mountain valleys of Pennsylvania run in a northerly direction, rather than east and west, thus making the route to Canada by way of the valleys to the north, then across the Finger Lake region of New York and across the Niagara, less arduous than the trek across the mountains of western Pennsylvania into Ohio.

Among the prominent spirits of the Ontario colony was Bishop Benjamin Eby, who, during the first half of the nineteenth century, served his people efficiently for many trying years as schoolteacher, preacher, bishop, and finally as publisher of many books and tracts, including his own brief history of the Mennonite Church, the first of its kind in America.

The total membership of the Mennonite and Amish churches of all branches in Ontario is somewhat less than 15,000.

CHAPTER 15

Mennonites and the Government

Relation to the State

The Pennsylvania Mennonites brought with them at the time of their arrival from the European homeland all of their inherited religious beliefs and traditional social practices. But while they were considerably hampered in Europe in the free exercise of their religious convictions, here under the free skies of a new world and the tolerant rule of the Quakers they were permitted the greatest liberty in following the dictates of conscience. Settling in large compact groups, speaking a foreign tongue, and conducting their own schools, isolated from the rest of the world socially, they formed self-sufficient economic and social units and religious congregations, free to conserve and perpetuate their distinctive pattern of life, without much likelihood of change far into the future. They created a little world of their own.

In the main, both because of their religious beliefs, and because of their distressing experiences with governmental agencies in Europe, they held themselves quite aloof in Pennsylvania from participation in the political affairs of their day, except occasionally when their votes were necessary to keep the nonresistant Quakers in control of the provincial Assembly, a control which the Quakers lost to their non-Quaker rivals in 1754.

In Germantown, which had the distinction of becoming, next to Philadelphia, the first village or borough in the province of Pennsylvania, the Mennonites and the Mennonite-Quakers, all of whom had inherited their opposition against participation in political life from a long European ancestry, became the first citizens of the borough, and its first political officials. At first, in the early and primitive political life of the village, so long as the village ordinances concerned themselves only with line fences and stray pigs, Mennonite officials seemingly were not altogether averse to holding office; but when, in the course of time, with the coming in of a larger non-Mennonite element, the jail and the whipping post had to be set up, Mennonites refused to serve as jurors, or as public officials, and to participate in the use of force. So Germantown lost its charter as a separate village largely because no one was found willing to hold office.

The Lancastrians, too, were without political ambitions, as is best evidenced by the fact that although rural Lancaster became almost solidly Mennonite in the course of time, yet during the period when the subdivisions of the county were being organized and named, not a single township, village, or any other subdivision was given a Mennonite name. Political organization, and later control, evidently was left entirely to the small group of Lutherans and Scotch-Irish.

But the Mennonites could not completely isolate themselves from the governmental control of even tolerant Pennsylvania. Only citizens could hold land in the province, and citizenship at first was conferred only upon those of English descent. All others must acquire this privilege through special petition to the provincial Assembly. The Germantown Mennonites early petitioned for and secured this privilege. The first petition from the Lancastrians appeared in 1729, and from the Amish in 1742.

The process of naturalization demanded the taking of the oath, and this, too, ran counter to one of the cardinal doctrines of the Mennonites. The provincial Assembly was generous in passing a law specifically exempting the Mennonites, Dunkards, and Amish from this obligation, substituting for the oath the simple affirmation. The same consideration was later granted the Mennonites in Maryland and Virginia.

Exemption from military service was also generally recognized, and conscientious scruples were always given careful consideration by those in authority. In Pennsylvania as well as in Maryland and Virginia, Quakers, Mennonites, and Dunkards were excused from militia musters common throughout the colonial period, in return usually for the payment of a small "fine."

It was their concern, however, for the preservation of their peace principles during the various Indian wars of the period that caused the Mennonites of the Skippack region to arrange with the Ephrata Brethren, in 1748, for the printing in German of their famous *Martyrs' Mirror.*

Jealous neighbors, however, were not always as considerate of the pacifist views of the Mennonites as were the governmental authorities. During the Revolutionary War especially, when partisanship ran high, and people were sharply divided into Tories or Loyalists and Patriots, all those who were wholeheartedly opposed to the war were banded as Tories and treated accordingly by those of the opposite party. In 1775, at the breaking out of the Revolutionary War, the Mennonites and Dunkers of Pennsylvania, true to their nonresistant convictions, sent to the provincial Assembly a joint petition stating their views on the question of war, and declaring

We have dedicated ourselves to serve all Men in every thing that can be helpful to the Preservation of Men's lives, but that we find no freedom in giving, or doing or assisting in anything by which Men's Lives are destroyed or hurt.

In the same year the Assembly found it necessary to warn certain disorderly elements in the northwestern part of Lancaster County against mob violence committed against the Mennonites for their refusal to join the militia companies then being organized, notwithstanding "their willingness to contribute cheerfully to the common cause otherwise than by taking up arms."

The whole adult male Mennonite population, seemingly, of the congregation near Saucon in Lehigh County was thrown into jail in 1778 and all their property confiscated, for their refusal to take the oath of allegiance required of all citizens after the Declaration of Independence was passed. There is a tradition among the Amish of Berks County that several were imprisoned in Reading for refusing to join the militia companies of that county.

Many of the Mennonite settlements of this period were made far out along the frontier, and thus subject to attack, especially at the time of the Indian wars. The destruction of the Northkill Amish settlement has been mentioned. There were other similar cases. In Page County, Virginia, during an Indian raid in 1766, the whole family of John Rhodes, a Mennonite minister, was cut down in cold blood.

We have already observed that the Mennonites were pioneers in the settling of our eastern frontiers. In 1683 they helped to found the first German colony in America, Germantown; in 1710 they were the earliest white settlers along the Pequea and Conestoga in Lancaster County; in 1727 they accompanied the first Germans from Lancaster County into the Shenandoah; and before the land along the headwaters of the Ohio in southwestern Pennsylvania had been officially opened up to settlement, they were found in that region; before 1800 they had formed the vanguard of the white settlers along the Grand River in Waterloo County, Ontario. In all these regions they were among the first to settle, and especially the first to form church organizations.

But it was not only as early settlers that the colonial Mennonites functioned as pioneers; they also pioneered in the promotion of numerous cultural and philanthropic achievements. Plockhoy's constitution of 1663 for the Mennonite colony on the Delaware, prohibiting slavery, has already been mentioned. Some years later, in 1688, another protest, usually spoken of as the first on record in America, was sent to the Philadelphia Quakers for their consideration and signed by one Mennonite, two Quakers who had originally been Mennonites, and one Lutheran pietist now also a Quaker. It is because of the varied religious complexion, no doubt, of these four signers that both Mennonites and Quakers are prone to claim credit for this early protest against this "traffik of Men-body which makes an ill report in all those countries of Europe where they hear of, that ye Quakers doe here handel men as they handel there ye cattle."

In the field of colonial education, too, Mennonites played far from an inconspicuous role. In Germantown they were the chief supporters of the private school taught by Pastorius, even before they had erected a meetinghouse. Throughout the colonial period schools were established in almost every Mennonite community. Among the famous colonial schoolmasters was the Mennonite, Christopher Dock, who, in 1750, wrote the *Schulordnung,* the first American treatise on the art of school management.

That the early Mennonites and their descendants played no small role in the later cultural and religious, as well as the economic development of the nation, is evidenced by the mere mention of a few names well known in both Pennsylvania and national life, such names as Hershey, Rittenhouse, Pennypacker, Overholt, Gorgas, Landes, Brubaker, Herr, Funk, Cunard.

CHAPTER 16

Westward Expansion and the New Immigrants

Pennsylvanians and Virginians Move West

The Mennonites, too, joined the general trek of the eastern land seekers, soon after the turn of the century, when the rich public lands beyond the Alleghenies were opened to settlement. They located in Ohio in 1798, with a group of Lancaster County Pennsylvanians, in what is now Fairfield County, near what soon became a new Lancaster, just ten years after the first white colony had been established at Marietta in the Northwest Territory. Other Mennonites from Pennsylvania and Virginia soon joined this settlement and helped to form the first Mennonite congregation in Ohio, with Henry Stemen, who came from Virginia in 1803, as the first Mennonite bishop in the state.

In 1807 another Pennsylvania colony was located in Mahoning and Columbiana counties, just across the state line from Pennsylvania. In 1811 a small Pennsylvania colony was settled in Stark County near Canton. A little earlier, in 1809, several Amish families from Somerset County, Pennsylvania, had established themselves along the Tuscarawas in the northeastern part of the state. But fearing an Indian invasion in the period just preceding the War of 1812 they were driven back to their Pennsylvania homes temporarily, only to return, however, after the war, with many others, where in the same region which is now Holmes and Tuscarawas counties they built up in course of time one of the largest Amish communities in America, still of the Old Order practice.

Mennonites seldom migrated to new localities as single families, but always in groups, and thus, new communities and church congregations always followed their westward trek. By the middle of the century flourishing Mennonite and Amish congregations appeared in Wayne, Champaign, Logan, Allen, Medina, Fulton, and other counties in Ohio; in northeastern New York; in northern Indiana, near Elkhart and Goshen; in central Illinois between Bloomington and Peoria; in southeastern Iowa, chiefly in Johnson and Washington counties; and after the Civil War in such western states beyond the Mississippi as Missouri, Kansas, and Nebraska, almost always, like the westward course of empire in general, in a straight line toward the setting sun. By 1880-1900 they reached the farthest west in Oregon south of Portland, near Salem and Albany.

A New Immigrant Tide

The economic distress and fear of further military oppression which followed the long period of the Napoleonic wars set in motion another wave of emigration to the land of freedom among the Mennonites of central Europe, who suffered most from these wars.

THE SWISS. The first to seek escape from their hardships were the Swiss. As early as 1817 a certain Benedict Schrag appeared with his family in Wayne County, Ohio. Others followed, largely from the Jura hills in the western end of the Canton of Berne, but some also from the Emmenthal region, until several flourishing congregations had been established near Dalton. In 1833 Michael Neuenschwander moved his family farther west to the banks of the Riley, in Putnam County, to found the large community at present near Bluffton, but at that time still a primitive wilderness. In 1838 Daniel Baumgartner started the colony at Berne, Indiana. All these communities at the time were located on the fringe of white settlements, much of the land being still purchased directly from the government land office. Large and prosperous congregations have since developed in all these settlements. The largest is the one at Berne, Indiana, consisting at present of some twelve hundred members, the largest Mennonite congregation in America. The majority of these Swiss have since affiliated with the General Conference branch of the denomination.

THE AMISH. A large contingent of Amish began to arrive almost at the same time, largely from Alsace and Lorraine, then still under French domination. The Amishman who led this migration was Christian Augsburger, an Alsatian, who in the course of a land-seeking tour through the Ohio Valley in 1818 ascended the Miami as far as present Butler County. Well pleased with the region about the

94

present village of Trenton, he returned the next year with five other families to begin the first foreign Amish community of this period. Others followed, but this pioneer congregation never grew large, although later in the early years of the general Amish migration it remained for a time a convenient distributing point and a way station for many of the immigrants, who tarried here for a while on their way to the cheaper lands farther west.

Nearly as early, in 1822, another Amish land seeker, Christian Nafziger, a Bavarian, arrived in Waterloo County, Canada, by way of New Orleans and Lancaster County. He returned to Europe, but after four years came back again to find that in 1824 an Amish colony of Alsatians and some Bavarians had founded the first Amish settlement in Canada, near the Mennonite colony which had been located there some years before. This Amish community has grown very large.

Beginning in the early thirties, and lasting until the fifties, three separate Amish communities, mostly from Alsace and Lorraine, had been established in northeastern New York, northwestern Ohio, and central Illinois, respectively. The congregations near Croghan, New York, with a present membership of nearly 900 have remained somewhat aloof; the one in Fulton County, Ohio, has expanded into a flourishing community of about 2,500 members, active in Mennonite affairs; while the Illinois settlement, the largest of the three, has developed into a number of prosperous communities throughout central Illinois totaling about 7,000 members. All of these original settlements have in turn furnished many members for daughter colonies in more recent years. Smaller Amish settlements of this same stock have been established in Stark County and Wayne County, Ohio, and north of Fort Wayne, Indiana. Another larger settlement was made in Washington and Henry counties in Iowa, with daughter settlements in Nebraska.

BAVARIANS. A little later, largely because of the economic uncertainties in Germany and the political upheavals of such revolutionary years as 1830 and 1848, a number of Bavarian and Palatinate Mennonites likewise sought refuge in America. Among the early individuals from this group to arrive here was Jacob Krehbiel, from the well-known Mennonite village of Weierhof, who in 1831 initiated a small congregation at Clarence Center, New York, not far from the Pennsylvania Mennonite community there. Later two entire Bavarian

95

congregations migrated en masse, Maxweiler and Eichstock, most of whom at first located in southeastern Iowa. Other small groups located in Ashland County, Ohio, and in Cleveland. Both of these latter, however, have long since disappeared as Mennonite congregations, while most of the Iowa group soon moved to Summerfield, Illinois, and later to Halstead, Kansas.

THE HESSIANS. In the meantime a number of Hessian families from Hesse-Darmstadt, Germany, formed several scattered communities—Butler County, Ohio; McLean and Putnam counties, Illinois; and a few scattered families in Waterloo County, Ontario.

A DUTCH CONGREGATION. In 1853 a party of fifty-two Dutch Mennonites from the last Dutch conservative congregation at Balk, Holland, because of their opposition to military service, and their reluctance to follow their more liberal-minded Dutch brethren in discarding the historic Mennonite doctrines, left their native land and settled near Elkhart, Indiana, where they later affiliated with the (old) Mennonites, and now form a part of the Salem congregation.

Judging entirely from the membership of the present congregations that grew out of all these early Amish and Mennonite settlements throughout the country, a rough estimate at this date of arrivals from Europe between 1817 and 1860 would be about as follows: Amish, 1,500; Swiss, 1,200; Bavarian Mennonites, 250; Hessians, 200; Dutch Mennonites, 52. These figures comprised the entire population including children, not merely the baptized members.

CHAPTER 17

The Coming of the Mennonites from Russia

The largest migration of Mennonites from Europe to America was that of the Russians, who came in two waves, the first during the ten-year period from 1874 to 1884, and the second from 1923 to 1930.

Escape from Military Service, 1874-80

In 1870 the Czar of Russia decided to follow the example of the German emperor in introducing universal military service in his empire without any special exemption for the Mennonites and the other German colonists who had settled in southern Russia under the reign of Catherine the Great one hundred years earlier with the definite promise of such exemption. The Mennonites became greatly disturbed at this threat to their peace principles. Even though the Czar later, as a result of repeated petitions sent to the imperial court by the Mennonites for the preservation of these privileges, finally promised to substitute forestry and other noncombatant service in lieu of regular army duty, about one third of the entire Mennonite body, fearful for the future, decided to migrate to America.

Fortunately for the Russian Mennonites there was still plenty of cheap land available in America for industrious and peace-loving foreigners; both Canada and the United States still welcomed desirable immigrants. The frontier line of settlements at this time, where cheap lands could be had, extended south from Winnipeg, through the western edge of the Red River Valley in Dakota territory, down through the middle of Nebraska and Kansas to the Indian Territory on the south. Here there was still plenty of land—free land, homestead, and railroad lands in almost limitless quantities, almost for the mere asking anxiously awaiting the settler. It was this frontier line that was recommended to their America-bent brethren for future homes by the special committee of twelve commissioners that the

Russian churches had sent out to spy out the "promised land" in 1873.

The inducements offered these prospective immigrants by both the Canadian and our own western state governments were most generous. Canada especially was exceedingly anxious to procure these industrious farmers for her western provinces, and offered most liberal concessions. She set aside for Mennonite occupation in Manitoba, which was still a primitive prairie wilderness with scarcely more than one thousand white inhabitants in the whole province, a solid block of seventeen townships, offering each head of a family 160 acres free, a large degree of local political autonomy, complete control over their own schools in their own language, and above all, complete military exemption, privileges as liberal as those granted them by Catherine the Great in Russia one hundred years earlier.

The United States government offered no special concessions to the newcomers, but the land departments and the railroad companies with large areas of land awaiting settlers did. The Santa Fe Railroad Company through Kansas was especially active, sending her colonization agent, C. B. Schmidt, to Russia to present the claims of the Sunflower State to the prospective immigrants. The Canadian government, likewise, sent William Hespeler for the same purpose. Nebraska, Kansas, and Minnesota eagerly passed legislation exempting Mennonites from militia service.

The American Mennonites also were generous in helping their Russian brethren to find new homes on the western prairies. Aid committees were organized in Pennsylvania, Ontario, and the Middle West to help the newcomers every step of the way, by lending them money, giving them temporary shelter along the way, and directing them to their new homes. The Canadian government lent them $100,000.00 on security furnished by the (old) Mennonites in Ontario, every cent of which was repaid in due time. Aided and directed by these helping agencies the Russian Mennonites arrived in 1874, 1875, 1876 by shipload along the eastern ports, and were transported to their western homes by the trainload. By 1880 some eight thousand had located in Manitoba, south of Winnipeg, and about ten thousand on the western prairies about Newton, Kansas, Yankton, South Dakota, Mountain Lake, Minnesota, and in smaller groups near Lincoln, Nebraska. Prominent leaders in organizing assistance for the settlement of the Russians in America were J. F. Funk, Elkhart, Indiana, J. Y. Shantz, Kitchener, Ontario, and Amos Herr, Lancaster, Pennsylvania.

Early pioneer life on the raw prairies was not without its hardships. The low prices following the panic of 1873 were perhaps a blessing in disguise, however, since for some years the new arrivals had little to sell, but much to buy, and so the low prices then prevailing were not altogether a disadvantage. But the meager farm equipment for the first years, life in uncomfortable sod houses, grasshopper plagues, hot winds, and occasional prairie fires often made the early years lean and uncertain. In course of time, however, all the settlements, both in Canada and in the United States, grew into outstandingly prosperous farming communities.

Being a religious people, determined that their faith should be preserved for their children, the Russian Mennonites organized churches and established schools from the start. All the divisions of the church known in Russia were imported to America. By far the largest portion of the settlers in the United States came from the Molotschna colony in Russia, while the Manitoba settlement was made up largely from the Old Colony, or Chortitz, and the Kleine Gemeinde group. The Mennonite Brethren were few and scattered, and for some years unorganized. The Krimmer Brethren were the only group in the United States to reproduce the farm village type of settlement, which they called Gnadenau.

The Russian immigrants for many years clung tenaciously to the German language, but World War I practically drove the use of the German out of the public and private schools in our own country. The western Mennonites finally reconciled themselves to the loss of their native tongue as a means of instruction in their schools; but not so their conservative Old Colony brethren in Manitoba, to whom there was a very close connection between their language and the preservation of their religious faith. Rather than submit to the Manitoba laws after the war, banning the German language from the schools, most of the Old Colonists, and some of the slightly less conservative Sommerfelders, decided to migrate to some other country where they might still preserve the use of their native tongue. About eight thousand of these from Manitoba and Saskatchewan left for Mexico in 1922, and about two thousand, a few years later, for the Gran Chaco in Paraguay. In both of these settlements these tenderminded Mennonites were granted all the privileges denied them in Canada, but amid a social and economic environment that is far less promising than that of Canada.

Flight from Bolshevism, 1923-30

A second mass immigration wave to the New World from war-ridden Russia, and by far the largest migration of Mennonites ever to occur, was the flight of some twenty-five thousand famine-stricken Mennonites from the terrors of pestilence, famine, banditry, and religious persecution that followed in the wake of the political and social revolution of 1917. For the native Slavic Russians, who were caught in the tragedies of the Russian revolution, there was no hope of escape; but for the German-speaking Mennonites, of original Dutch stock, who had back of them a long tradition of trekking from one country to another for conscience' sake, and whose many brethren in Holland and Germany as well as in America, were vitally interested in their rescue, the possibility of escape was not entirely hopeless. Following a visit made to these countries in 1920 by a delegation of Russian Mennonites for the purpose of exploring the possibilities of outside help from their western European and American brethren, a movement was started which, in the years between 1923 and 1930, brought to America, North and South, approximately twenty-five thousand Russian Mennonites who had been deprived in their homeland of their prosperous farms, fine homes, and their religious liberties, by the regime that in the meantime had gotten possession of the machinery of the Russian government.

The delegation of 1920 had found during their visit here that the doors to further immigration to the United States had been closed by the quota law; and that Canada, too, had barred the doors to Mennonites in particular by an earlier Order in Council passed shortly after World War I. Mexico, because of its own revolution, was not given much consideration by the Russian delegates. Owing, however, to the persevering efforts of a newly organized Mennonite Board of Colonization, and especially its chief promoter, David Toews of Rosthern, Saskatchewan, and the sympathetic aid given by the Prime Minister MacKenzie King, who had in his youth been a neighbor at Kitchener, Ontario, of the (old) Mennonites of Waterloo County, and the generous support of the Canadian Pacific Railroad Company, the objectionable Order in Council was repealed. Soon the doors opened wide for the reception, during the years immediately following, of some twenty-three thousand poverty-stricken Mennonites, who were safely transported to the "land of promise" in Western Canada, largely

100

on credit advanced by the Canadian Pacific Railroad Company. Had it not been for the splendid record of payments of the Mennonite immigrants of 1874-80, this could not have been done.

In 1929, another group of about four thousand were able to escape the Red Terror, many of them this time from the Siberian settlements. These were the successful remnant of some ten or more thousands of German colonists who in that year had descended upon Moscow, lured there by false reports that the way to America was opened, grasping at any straw that held out the nearest chance of escape. With the help this time of the German government itself, which immediately interested itself in the plight of these Moscow refugees, the personal concern even of President von Hindenburg, who secured an appropriation of six million marks from the Reichstag, the German and Dutch Mennonites, the German Red Cross, and the united efforts of the American Mennonite Central Committee, about one thousand of these unfortunates were able to join their Canadian brethren even though the doors here had again been closed to further immigration because of the economic depression that had seized the world at that time. About seventeen hundred were transported to Paraguay near the earlier Canadian colony which had been established in 1926, at the expense of the Mennonite Central Committee; while the German government was responsible for the settlement of about an equal number in southern Brazil on raw land owned by a large German land company. The Paraguayan settlers were offered the same liberal religious and civil privileges offered to the earlier neighboring Canadian colony of Menno, but those located in Brazil were granted no special concessions.

E. Origin, History, and Distinctive Contributions of the Various Mennonite Branches

Introduction

There is perhaps no other religious denomination that in proportion to its numbers has been separated into so many different branches as the American Mennonites. This is the result of several causes. First of all the Mennonites had always been individualistic in their religious thinking, and congregational in their church government. While the Catholic church member may depend on his priest as the source of his spiritual instruction, and the members of the other state churches upon their university doctors of theology and ecclesiastical authorities, the Mennonites find their instruction by themselves in the Bible. This independent, personal search for the Truth makes for a variety of interpretations. The loosely organized congregational type of church government, which leaves each congregation a complete and independent ecclesiastical unit with no obligation to any other religious governing body, necessarily also makes for variety rather than unity. It must be said, however, that recent generations have brought about a development in the direction of conference supervision and control of congregations in some groups.

The American Mennonites, too, came to this country at different periods of time, and from widely scattered European regions, where in the course of centuries each settlement or national group had developed differences in social and religious practices. These differences were all imported into America, where again they were perpetuated in isolated groups with but slight religious intercourse with one another. The Swiss who came to Ohio in 1817 did not speak the same language, nor use the same hymnbooks, nor practice the same form of worship, as did the Hessians who came to Illinois in 1840, or the Russian Mennonites who located in Kansas in 1875. It took many years of living together in America before these all agreed to join the General Conference movement. The Amish division of 1693-97 and all of the divisions among the Russian churches occurred in Europe, and continued their separate existence here.

It must be remembered, too, that under the free skies of America any aggressive leader can get a following, no matter how extreme or how peculiar his views. Several of the small factions among the Mennonites, for the most part now forgotten, were of this character. Most of the others represented honest differences of opinion. Not all people are of like temperament. Some are especially susceptible to emotional appeals; others to intellectual emphases. This psychological difference has been the cause of several divisions within the church, particularly during the middle of the century when for some years there was a wave of religious fervor and evangelistic effort pervading more or less all the Protestant church bodies of America.

The Mennonites in the main were never given over to much emotionalism in their religious worship. They took their religion seriously as a normal experience, sometimes perhaps as a matter of fact. Children were taught the faith of the fathers and the ways of the church. In the course of years as a result of good parental example and catechetical instruction they arrived at a state of realization of the need of a personal Saviour in their lives. Worship consisted of a more or less formal service, and few attempts were made to stir the depths of individual religious feeling. In the main, Mennonite convictions were sincere, deep, and abiding. This was the religious attitude of the majority of the Mennonites in America up to the middle of the century, when as a result of the religious awakening throughout the land they, too, were somewhat affected by this general movement here and there. Among the Mennonite branches who today owe at least a part of their distinctive doctrines to this cause, and perhaps somewhat also to the later revival movement led by Moody and others, may be mentioned the Mennonite Brethren in Christ (now the United Missionary Church), the Mennonite Brethren imported from Russia, and the Evangelical Mennonites. Baptist influence in Russia was marked on the Mennonite Brethren.

The American Mennonites, too, like many other early distinctively religious groups, Quakers, Dunkers, Puritans, Methodists, and certain wings of the Baptist Church, all through their history have been rather conservative and slow to drop well-tried religious practices and social usages in favor of newer and untried methods and forms as these made their appearance from time to time. Since there are two extremes to every movement, social or religious, there were always those among the Mennonites who thought the church was moving too slowly, others who thought it moved too fast. And so as

103

the social order changed, several new wings of the church made their appearance. Among the new ventures that became sources of controversy were the use of the English language in worship, Sunday schools, prayer meetings, evening meetings, the mission enterprise, new and changing styles of dress, the use of new inventions, and a more liberal affiliation with the non-Mennonite social and religious world.

It will thus be seen that it is not usually differences in fundamental Christian beliefs nor Mennonite doctrines but rather variations in certain lesser social and religious practices or emphases that account for the twenty or so varieties of Mennonitism in America. These different branches in the next chapter are classified as to their original sources as Pennsylvania Mennonites, Amish, and Russo-German Mennonites.

CHAPTER 18

Pennsylvania Mennonites and Their Descendant Groups

The Reformed Mennonites (1812)

The first permanent division among the American Mennonites was the branch later spoken of as the Reformed Mennonites, founded by John Herr of Lancaster County in 1812. The origin of this division is somewhat obscure. John Herr had never been a Mennonite, though his father Francis Herr had been, having been expelled, however, for reasons no longer definitely known. John, together with several of his friends, sympathizers, no doubt, of his father, took up the cause of Francis, formed a new congregation, baptizing and rebaptizing one another.

Herr and his followers found no fault with Menno Simons and his teaching, charging rather that the Lancaster church had departed from the ways of their leaders, especially from the life of nonconformity with the outside world which Menno taught and practiced in his own day. The true church, they maintained, must be closely held together and insulated against the outside religious and social world, a position which this group still rigidly follows, though they seemingly enter freely into the professional and business life of today.

The Reformed Mennonites, sometimes called "New Mennonites" in Lancaster County, maintain a strict discipline within their own ranks by means of the practice of avoidance. They have largely retained their early conservatism, and have not followed most of the other branches into progressive church enterprises, such as Sunday schools, evangelistic meetings, young people's meetings, and mission work. They still demand extreme plainness of dress, and maintain an untrained, unpaid ministry. They have grown very slowly. Their total baptized membership today is a little over eight hundred, still principally in Lancaster County, though there are a few congregations in several other states.

The Oberholtzer Group (1847)

The next separation among the Pennsylvania Mennonites occurred in 1847, in what was known as the Franconia District of the (old) Mennonite Church. The Mennonites at this time in this compact settlement were quite conservative in their religious practices. Unlike the Herr incident, which was a conservative reaction and involved only one family in the beginning, this movement was inaugurated by a liberal wing of the church, and included several ministers, one bishop, and a number of laymen from most of the twenty-two congregations of the district, as well as several entire congregations, about one third of the entire membership.

The withdrawing group, led by a young minister named John H. Oberholtzer, organized a new body on October 28, 1847, under the name "Eastern Pennsylvania District." The controversy concerned itself not with fundamental questions of theology, but rather with matters of religious and social usages. Judging from the church policies adopted by the new wing of the denomination in the years immediately following, it seems that the main demand was for a more tolerant attitude toward the outside world on such questions as outside marriage, open communion, removal of dress restrictions, a limited use of the courts in settling civil disagreements, and other similar practices previously forbidden.

The new group also early adopted a progressive program of church work. The first American Mennonite church paper, the *Religiöser Botschafter,* was founded by Oberholtzer at Milford Square in 1852. Not much later Oberholtzer also started religious instruction in his church for young people (although the first real Sunday school was not begun until 1853 in another congregation), and the first missionary society in 1865. Oberholtzer and his followers later played an important role in the formation of the General Conference Mennonite Church. In 1858 a faction led by William Gehman formed the Evangelical Mennonites. Two other small divisions occurred about the same time.

106

The Church of God in Christ, Mennonite (1858)

[The following account was prepared by Frank H. Wenger, and is used by his kind permission.—Editor.]

This church, a branch of the Mennonites, was organized in 1858 in Wayne County, Ohio, with John Holdeman of New Pittsburg, Ohio, as leader.

The restoration of primitive Christianity was the watchword of Holdeman and his followers, endeavoring to restore those teachings of the early fathers that had been abandoned by most branches of the church. All questions were decided upon a Scriptural and primitive basis, after much prayer and a careful study of the Word of God. Space does not permit to quote Holdeman's own account of his experiences and his powerful inward convictions as to his call and ordination of God to be a minister of the Gospel. Step by step the Lord led the way. When he and his group came to the question of naming the organization, they again turned to the Scriptures and found that a Bible institution should have a Biblical name; hence, Church of God in Christ, Mennonite.

Members are admitted through baptism, by pouring, after producing evidence of true repentance, forgiveness of sins, and the new birth. In practice the church is conservative, and endeavors to be separate from the world in all things that do not tend to spiritual life, holding the Old and New Testaments as their rule of faith. The 18 and 33 articles of faith (as found in the *Martyrs' Mirror*) are recognized as sound doctrine, and a spiritual discipline is accordingly exercised for the purity of the church and the salvation of God's people. The church holds a twofold ministry, viz., first, ministers or elders (who may differ in gifts but officially are all equal), who minister to the spiritual needs of the church; second, deacons, who minister to the financial needs of the poor and the church. Both are chosen from among the laity and ordained into their respective office by the laying on of hands.

In the beginning the church increased slowly, but the spirit of evangelism burned in the hearts of the brethren, whereupon qualified brethren were ordained and sent out to preach the old time religion— "The Gospel of Christ which is the power of God unto salvation to everyone that believeth." Thus congregations have been organized in fourteen different states, three provinces of Canada, and one in Mexico, comprising a baptized membership of over 7,000 in 1963.

The Old Order Mennonites (1871-1901)

This branch, also sometimes known as the "Wisler" group, is composed of four small groups, who, at different times (1871-1901) and places (Indiana, Ohio, Ontario, Pennsylvania), withdrew from the parent body because of opposition to the adoption of certain "new things."

The first of the new groups to be formed was the Wisler wing of the Mennonite congregation at Yellow Creek, in Elkhart County, Indiana, in 1871. At that time Sunday schools, English preaching, protracted meetings, and four-part singing were just beginning to make their appearance in church worship and in the Mennonite churches of Indiana. Jacob Wisler, one of the earliest bishops in the state, opposed these foreign innovations in his congregation. The majority of his congregation disagreeing with him, he withdrew, and formed a separate congregation, known in this region as the Wisler church. Similar divisions occurred in the churches in Medina and Columbiana counties, Ohio.

A little later, in the late eighties (1889), a similar conservative movement appeared in the Ontario Conference district at several places, chiefly in Woolwich Township in Waterloo County. From this center several settlements were affected. In the early nineties Bishop Jonas Martin led a conservative division in the Lancaster Conference. In 1901 a similar breach occurred in one of the congregations in Rockingham County, Virginia.

These four groups, having much in common, and otherwise isolated, finally joined their forces in a working fellowship and are now spoken of as the Old Order Mennonites, though this name is not officially recognized by any of them. This group still practices a strict church discipline through the medium of avoidance. They are very plain in their dress, and oppose most of the progressive forms of church worship which caused their first withdrawal from the parent church. They are quite similar in their general practices and attitudes to the manner of life and customs of the Old Order Amish, except that they do not have the same dress and do not require the wearing of the beard. Their baptized membership in 1963 was 6,866, distributed over about fifty congregations in Ohio, Indiana, Ontario, and Pennsylvania.

The Mennonite Brethren in Christ (1873)

This wing of the Mennonite denomination, likewise, was the result of a series of amalgamations of four small kindred groups, three of which had seceded from the main body for similar reasons, namely, the desire for a more evangelistic and warmer type of religious life. The fourth group was a secession from an earlier body that had been influenced largely in its formation by a former Mennonite.

"New Mennonites" was the name assumed by a small division of Canadian Mennonites, formed about 1850 under the leadership of Daniel Hoch, an aggressive minister in the congregation in Lincoln County, Ontario. Hoch, however, after having led this group out of the main body, did not follow them into their later affiliations, but became one of the founders of the General Conference Church.

"Reformed Mennonites," not to be confused with the Herr following of the same name in Lancaster County, was the group formed in 1874 by the union of two other groups that had withdrawn from the old church some time before—one in Elkhart County, Indiana, and the other in Bruce County and Waterloo County, Ontario. Daniel Brenneman was a fellow minister in the Yellow Creek congregation with Bishop Jacob Wisler above-mentioned, and favored all the progressive church measures which his bishop opposed. Between these two extremes the main body of the Yellow Creek congregation steered a middle course, and Brenneman too, committed to practices somewhat too progressive for the middle group, soon found himself leading a small division of sympathizers out of the congregation.

In the meantime, a movement along similar lines and under similar circumstances had taken place among several congregations in Ontario, under the leadership of minister Solomon Eby, who according to his own testimony, having been ordained to the ministry by lot in 1858, was not "happily converted" until 1869. He stressed especially the need of a more "definite experience" in the act of conversion and a freer expression of the religious spirit in the form of frequent prayer meetings and evangelistic services. Brenneman, after several visits with the Canadian group, finally joined the Eby following in the formation in 1874 of the Reformed Mennonites.

The third of these co-operating groups was the Evangelical Mennonites, founded in 1858 by William Gehman, an early follower of the Oberholtzer wing in Pennsylvania, but later also dismissed from the Eastern District Conference because of a difference of opinion over the question of a more fervid form of worship by means of prayer meetings and evangelistic services. The fourth, and non-Mennonite, contingent of this combination was a group of the Brethren in Christ in Ohio, who, as early as 1838, had seceded from the parent group.

These four small bodies, all with a more or less direct Mennonite origin, and with quite similar beliefs and practices, by a series of amalgamations at different times united to form the Mennonite Brethren in Christ. The unification was completed in 1883. In 1947 all except the Pennsylvania Conference of this group voted to adopt United Missionary Church as their denominational name. The Pennsylvania branch retained the name of Mennonite Brethren in Christ until 1959, when they became known as the Bible Fellowship Church.

This branch of the church still holds to many of the distinctive doctrines of the parent body. During World War II, however, less than five per cent of its drafted men chose alternative service. And stressing, as it does, the necessity of a very definite sense of conversion and a decided conviction of sin, as well as a certain assurance of salvation as a condition of membership, they emphasize the necessity of giving expression to these experience in their public worship.

According to J. A. Huffman, a prominent minister of this branch, the Mennonite Brethren in Christ had

> no certain prescribed mode of dress, but they always insisted on modesty in matters of dress, and a separation from the world. In the practice of baptism, the church insists upon single immersion. Membership in secret oath-bound societies is forbidden. Emphasis has been and continues to be placed upon a definite experience of conversion, and a subsequent or a second crisis experience, that of sanctification, and the Spirit-filled life.

The church carries on a strong missionary program, both foreign and home. Many of the small congregations found in this branch first began as mission stations in cities and small towns. It has perhaps more non-Mennonite family names in its membership than any other wing of the denomination. During the past generation, moreover, its extra-denominational associations have had an increasingly Wesleyan-Holiness-Fundamentalist rather than a Mennonite orientation. The change in name and the fact that no delegates have been appointed to the Mennonite World Conference are further illustrations of this development, indicating that for practical purposes the group no longer considers itself as within the Mennonite family. The entire membership today is approximately thirteen thousand, found largely in Ohio, Indiana, Ontario, and Pennsylvania.

CHAPTER 19

The Mennonite Church
[Sometimes Called the "Old" Mennonites]

The defections and separations from the parent body as just described, to both the right and the left sides, left the main trunk still the largest body in the denomination, which we shall here arbitrarily call the (old) Mennonites, though that is not the official name of the group, and is not recognized by them. This main trunk, which, until they were joined by the Amish Mennonites in the late nineties and after, was almost exclusively of Pennsylvania Mennonite origin, was not greatly influenced at the time by the two extreme tendencies. They steered rather a moderate course in church practice, and, although they remained conservative in their religious activities, they were not so wedded to the old ways of doing things that they kept their eyes closed to all progressive methods just because they were new.

As in every social movement, progress here, too, must be credited largely to a small group of forward-looking leaders, chief among whom during this period was John F. Funk, a young Pennsylvania layman, who entered Chicago just before the Civil War to engage in the lumber business. Becoming deeply interested in religious work and being associated for a time with D. L. Moody in Sunday-school activities, Funk soon gave up his business interests to establish a printing and publishing enterprise for the special benefit of the Mennonite reading public. In 1864 he founded the *Herald of Truth,* and its German counterpart, the *Herold der Wahrheit.* A few years later he removed his publishing establishment to Elkhart, Indiana, where it finally became known as the Mennonite Publishing Company. For the next fifty years this publishing house, still privately owned, furnished not only the (old) Mennonites but many of the other smaller groups as well much of their religious literature, including translations of the voluminous works of Menno Simons, the big *Martyrs' Mirror,* the two church papers already mentioned, Sunday-school supplies, hymnbooks, and numerous tracts and books of a religious and denominational character. Needless to say, the Mennonite Publishing Company, and the Mennonite congregation that arose out of it at Elkhart, became a vital force in promoting progressive church work throughout the whole denomination.

Funk's church papers persistently advocated the cause of Sunday schools, missions, evangelistic efforts, and other progressive church enterprises at a time when the majority of the (old) Mennonites were still decidedly opposed to any departure from the ways of the fathers. Progressive church leaders, here and there, also found the pages of these papers open for the expression of their individual views on many a vital religious question.

Another leader was a young Virginia schoolteacher and preacher by the name of John S. Coffman, who was brought to Elkhart as assistant editor of the *Herald of Truth*. Coffman, who was a young man of unusual charm, of an attractive personality and amiable disposition, with high ideals, an able public speaker, well able to use the English language at a time when German was still in vogue in nearly all of the (old) Mennonite pulpits of the Middle West, better educated than most of the Mennonite preachers of his day, and sincerely devoted to the church, did not confine himself solely to the editorial desk. In the eighties and nineties he visited numerous congregations, both in the United States and in Ontario, to hold some of the earliest evangelistic services in this particular branch of the church. Young people, especially, were attracted by the winning personality of this unusual preacher; and everywhere he visited, a new interest was aroused in more progressive church work. Talented young men here and there were influenced to dedicate their lives to a career of usefulness in the mission field, in the schoolroom, and in the ministry.

Among the new ventures in church work which were introduced during the next fifty years, with considerable opposition in many quarters, were Sunday schools, the use of the English language in worship, evening services and evangelistic meetings, young people's work, missions, education for the young people, and training for the ministry.

The first of these innovations was the Sunday-school movement, which had made its appearance in a few isolated congregations some time before, but had not yet come to be generally accepted. By the late eighties, Sunday schools had come to be accepted quite generally throughout the church, accompanied by a deeper interest in evangelization. In 1882 the Indiana-Michigan Conference appointed an evangelization committee. Soon after a Book and Tract Society was organized at Elkhart, to be followed later by benevolent and mission boards. In 1892, in the Clinton Frame Church near Goshen, was held the first of a series of Sunday-school conventions, which by giving the young people from the various congregations throughout the country an opportunity of discussing their common religious and social problems, greatly aided the forward movement of the church. The first home mission was founded in Chicago in 1893; and the first foreign mission in India in 1898. The present Mennonite Board of Missions and Charities was organized in 1905 as an amalgamation of two earlier boards.

The interest in higher education was also given increased attention. In 1895 John S. Coffman and Jonas S. Hartzler, among other forward-looking Mennonites from northern Indiana, organized an association which took over a private normal school that had been established one year before under the name of "The Elkhart Institute," and converted it into an academy and Bible school to "provide a higher education for our young people without exposing them to the dangerous influences surrounding so many of the schools of our country." In 1903 this school was transferred to Goshen and called Goshen College. In 1906 the control of the college was placed in the hands of a board of trustees representing the different district conferences of the church, called the Mennonite Board of Education. Other such schools of higher learning have since been established at Hesston, Kansas (1909), and at Harrisonburg, Virginia (1917).

The (old) Mennonites also conduct a number of charitable institutions, several homes for the aged, children's homes and hospitals, as well as numerous mission stations, both foreign and home. Since the close of World War I also they have been active in relief work in foreign lands.

Theologically and doctrinally, this branch of the denomination is still quite conservative, officially holding to the Dortrecht Confession of Faith, without, however, following it blindly. The practice of avoidance, advocated by their confession, has never been accepted by the American Mennonites, as it has been by the Amish. Church leaders still stress the doctrine of nonconformity, which was once defined by Daniel Kauffman as follows:

A Scriptural doctrine requiring separation between the church and the world. Believers, having accepted Christ as their personal Saviour, have hereby renounced their former adherence to the world with its sinful lusts and follies, and are therefore, not to be conformed to the world in business methods, in political affiliations, in methods of living, in dress, etc., their attitude being described in the language of inspiration as "unspotted from the world."

Modesty in dress is still encouraged; for both men and women, although congregations differ somewhat in the strictness with which this principle is put into practice.

Meetinghouses among the (old) Mennonites are still simple but substantial. Instrumental music is not commonly used in worship.

In some areas the ministry is still selected from among the local membership, though the tendency is away from this practice. In 1937 Daniel Kauffman listed in his *Mennonite Cyclopedic Dictionary* the following church issues which he considered important:

Spiritual life as distinguished from mere church membership; Christian orthodoxy as opposed to liberalism; a free ministry as opposed to a salaried system; separation of church and state; separation between the church and the world; freedom from the unequal yoke with unbelievers; nonresistance or peace as opposed to carnal warfare; organized secretism; labor unionism; the insurance problem; the dress question; the amusement heresy; evangelism and missionary activities; Christian federation vs. Christian unity; Scriptural discipline; eschatology.

Most of these are still live issues in the (old) Mennonite group, even if the official position of the church may have shifted in a few cases.

In church government the (old) Mennonites are still basically congregational, but in some areas the conference has assumed prominence as a governing body. The term *bishop,* as used traditionally by Mennonites, has a different connotation from that of most other church bodies. The minister thus named was formerly the only one in the congregation who had full power to perform all the religious functions of the congregation, such as baptism, marriage, and communion. Earlier the bishop was responsible only for his own congregation, although in a few places he might have six or seven congregations in his charge. Today innovations are being made in this traditional pattern of ordination. The tendency is to give more and more responsibility to the minister and to make the bishop an administrator, who acts in an advisory capacity for a number of ministers in a given area.

As of 1963 there are now twenty-one conferences in the Mennonite Church, which include the Argentine and Puerto Rican conferences and the Mennonite Church in India. These conferences are sometimes merely advisory, with no power to legislate for the individual congregations except to refuse membership to a congregation in the conference in case of difference of opinion on religious questions. But in most cases they have become legislative.

In the late nineties of the past century a number of the Amish Mennonite congregations of the Middle West began to co-operate with the Mennonites in their conference activities. From 1915 to 1925 these groups merged with the Mennonite conferences, thus giving up their distinctive Amish name, and greatly strengthening the Mennonite group, which had never been numerically strong in the Middle West, west of Indiana.

In 1898 the various district conferences west of the Alleghenies formed the Mennonite General Conference, which meets biennially. Some eastern conferences have as yet not seen fit to join wholeheartedly with this General Conference movement among the (old) Mennonites, although many of the individual ministers from all the districts attend with full participation in the General Conference sessions. This Mennonite General Conference is not to be confused with the General Conference Mennonite Church, which is another branch altogether.

The *Mennonite Yearbook* for 1966 gives the total baptized membership in the United States and Canada as over 88,000. The group has a large and successful publishing house at Scottdale, Pennsylvania. The *Gospel Herald* is the church organ.

CHAPTER 20

The Amish Groups

The Amish wing of the church also had its internal controversies during this period. As already seen, living as they did in separate isolated communities, they at first had little religious affiliation with their Mennonite brethren. Although the various Amish congregations remained independent without any binding conference connections, yet they all retained almost identical practices and customs, and regarded themselves as one spiritual body. Even the European Amish, largely from Alsace and Lorraine, who migrated to Ohio and Illinois in the early thirties and forties of the past century, had developed no distinctive differences by this time; they freely fellowshiped with their American Amish brethren. All still wore simple clothing, kept the customs of the forefathers, and practiced the Amish doctrine of avoidance; they spoke the same modified form of the south German dialect, worshiped only in homes, and sang from the same old *Ausbund*.

But by about 1850 slight variations began to appear among some of the widely scattered native Pennsylvanians as well as among the more recently immigrated congregations. On the one hand there was a tendency toward laxer practices of the old traditions, and on the other hand a strict insistence upon opposition to change.

It was for the purpose of harmonizing these various disagreements and bringing about a closer co-operation among the various communities that a series of general conferences of all the Amish congregations was called. These conferences met annually for a number of years, from 1862 to 1878, without accomplishing the purpose for which they were originally called. In fact, the final result was the crystallization of the entire American Amish body into three well-defined parties. On the one hand the congregation in McLean County, Illinois, and the Hessian congregation in Ohio, somewhat more tolerant in their church discipline than the others, lost interest in the conferences before the end, ceased to attend the later sessions, and began an independent career. On the other hand a goodly number of congregations, principally from the east and decidedly conservative, together with such as had never favored the conference idea, maintained all the good old customs of the fathers without the slightest change. These have since become known as the *"Old Order Amish."* Between these two extremes were left a considerable number including most of the Alsatian immigrant communities, and the Wayne, Champaign, and Logan County Pennsylvanians in Ohio, and part of the Elkhart County Pennsylvanians in Indiana, who occupied a middle position, followed a fairly moderate course, and later organized conferences. These later, as noted, merged with the Mennonites, thus losing their distinctive name and existence.

The Central Conference of Mennonites

This group, locally known for a long time as the "Stuckey people," had its origin in the Rock Creek congregation in McLean County, Illinois, in the early seventies. The bishop here was Joseph Stuckey, one of the most promising of the leaders in the entire church during this period, a man of strong personality, frequent contributor to the church papers, an able speaker and frequent visitor among the Amish congregations, and talented with more than ordinary organizing ability. Theologically he agreed in the main with the teachings of the church, but was somewhat more tolerant than many of his fellow ministers, and perhaps somewhat more lax in his church discipline. As a result he ceased to find happy fellowship with the other Amish churches after 1870.

Hence when in the late eighties these same Amish churches united with other congregations in Iowa and Nebraska to form a new conference, the Western District Amish Conference, the Rock Creek Church was not represented, and from that time the so-called Stuckey following was considered as a separate branch of the church. By this time, too, this congregation had introduced a number of innovations, had discarded largely the strict conventional dress regulations, and had assumed a more tolerant attitude toward fellowshiping with other religious bodies and the non-Mennonite world in general, so that it was quite out of step religiously with the conservative congregations, which for the most part had retained these practices.

Not only did Stuckey retain control of his own congregation during this controversy, but others soon joined his group. The Stuckey following grew gradually by additions from the other Amish congregations and by daughter colonies. In 1899 the Stuckey congregations, at that time twelve in number, united to form the Central Illinois Conference of Mennonites, in 1914 dropping the "Illinois" from its name, and in 1945 uniting with the General Conference Mennonite Church. In 1951 they numbered 3,252 members with twenty congregations. In that year they merged with the former Middle District Conference of the General Conference Mennonite Church, thus losing their identity as a group.

The Evangelical (Defenseless) Mennonite Church

Even before the separation of the Stuckey group, a more definite division had occurred in an Alsatian Amish congregation in Adams County, Indiana. This controversy arose over the issue of a more emotional form of religious worship, and an even more strict discipline than that exercised by the already well-disciplined Amish of that day. The origin of the Evangelical Mennonite Church (until 1948 known as Defenseless Mennonites) is perhaps best told in the words of their Church Manual, published in 1937.

"The Defenseless Mennonite Church had its origin through the direction of God and the instrumentality of the Holy Ghost, in the person of Henry Egly of Geneva, Indiana, an elder of the so-called 'Old Order Amish Mennonites,' who hitherto had not experienced a change of heart, was truly and happily converted, and at once introduced these means of grace into his church, insisting on a personal experience of forgiveness of sins and a change of heart of all those who wished to partake of the Lord's Supper. He also required rebaptism of those (but only those) who had not made this experience, before uniting with the church, believing that baptism was but the answer of a good conscience toward God.

"When he made his position known, one half of his congregation withdrew, and refused to have anything more to do with him. Of the other half of the congregation, about one half of the members had made a personal experience of salvation, either before they were baptized in the Old Church, or after they had been baptized. The remaining half of the members requested prayer that they, too, might see the Light and receive the experience of conversion and regeneration. This occurred in 1864-66.

This Egly movement also spread to several of the Amish congregations in Illinois, and to western Ohio. The entire membership today is about 2,500. Among the distinctive doctrines included in their confession of faith are found adoption, divine healing, and sanctification. In 1901 a section of the group withdrew to form the "Missionary Church Association."

The Amish Mennonites

As already indicated, between the progressive Stuckey group and the strictly conservative Old Order Amish group, there remained a middle and more moderate group, mostly from the Middle West, and of more recent Alsatian origin, who were not altogether averse to accommodating themselves to such new methods of church work as seemed necessary to promote the progress of the church. These new methods included such innovations as the Sunday school, mission enterprise, young people's meetings, the use of meetinghouses for worship, and also the discarding of older styles of dress. These moderate congregations finally assumed the name of Amish Mennonites, and beginning about 1882 formed themselves into regional conferences. Being identical with their Mennonite neighbors in religious belief and practice, they ultimately merged their religious efforts with those of the Mennonites. And so, by giving up their own identity and the name "Amish," they ended the breach between the two branches of the church which had kept them apart for two hundred years in Europe and America.

There are small groups, however, who retain in their name "Amish Mennonite." The largest of these groups at present is known as the Beachy Amish Mennonite Church, with a membership of about 3,000 in 1963. These are a group nearer to the Old Order Amish, but more progressive. They worship in meetinghouses, engage in mission work, favor Sunday schools, and sponsor a religious paper called *Herold der Wahrheit,* a part-German, part-English publication. They can be found in Pennsylvania, Ontario, Ohio, Indiana, Illinois, Iowa, Michigan, Virginia, Maryland, Georgia, Oklahoma, Arkansas, and New York.

The Old Order Amish

The various separations just described leave the main line of Amish still the largest division of this branch of the church, with customs and practices intact, with hardly a change since their arrival in America, now commonly spoken of as the Old Order Amish. They have a membership today in the United States and Ontario of about nineteen thousand, almost all descendants from the original Pennsylvanians, with a few from the more recent Alsatians. They are grouped in rather compact settlements across the country from Pennsylvania to Kansas—in Lancaster, Mifflin, and Somerset counties, Pennsylvania; Tuscarawas and Holmes counties, Ohio; Elkhart, Noble, Lagrange, and Howard counties, Indiana; Moultrie and Douglas counties, Illinois; Johnson and Washington counties, Iowa; Reno County, Kansas; with smaller settlements in Ontario and other regions.

The Old Order Amish still hold fast to the old customs and traditions, dressing severely plain, in styles common long ago, and forbidding the possession of most of the modern inventions, such as the automobile and telephone. They have no meetinghouses, church conferences, or other new church activities, and few Sunday schools. They are more devoted than their more liberal brethren to the old literature of the church, such as the writings of Menno Simons and the *Martyrs' Mirror*. Dirk Philips' *Enchiridion* is still read by them, largely because he is almost the only early Mennonite writer who pays special attention to the practice of avoidance, a disciplinary measure still strictly observed by the Old Order. The *Ausbund* is still the accepted hymnbook. It is not only the ancient customs and traditions that the Old Order Amish have preserved through the centuries; they have also preserved more faithfully than some of the other branches certain of the fundamental teachings of the fathers.

Although still most conservative in their social customs and religious practices, the members of this branch of the church are noted for their industry and frugality. The Amish are good farmers, usually having the best horses and cattle in their communities. They take care of their own needy and never become a public charge. They mind their own business, are devoted to their families, and are among the most peaceable and useful citizens of the country, though not the most progressive. The publicity often given them in the press and by certain writers of fiction seldom does them justice. A sympathetic and accurate description of their life and practices is found in a story called *Rosanna of the Amish,* by Joseph W. Yoder (1940), who as the son of one of their bishops in Mifflin County, Pennsylvania, was well qualified to speak for them.

In more recent times Clara Bernice Miller, a former member of the Beachy Amish, has written a novel entitled *The Crying Heart* (Herald Press, 1962), perhaps the most sympathetic attempt to describe the Amish church from within, through the medium of fiction.

CHAPTER 21

The Russo-German Mennonite Groups

The Russo-German Mennonites form a third group of branches among the American Mennonites. All of the major divisions among the Russian immigrants, having had their origin in Russia, were imported at the time of the immigration. Like the divisions among the Mennonites elsewhere, these among the Russians were not based on radically different views on questions of religious belief, but rather of religious practices resulting from living in widely separated and independent self-governing congregations, or from varying attitudes toward the outside world. Sometimes the depth of a religious emotion, in some cases merely the form of baptism, caused the division. The Manitoba immigrants came largely from the old Chortitza colony in Russia and its daughter colonies, all extremely conservative at the time of the immigration; while the settlers in the United States were mostly from the more progressive and tolerant Molotschna colony.

The General Conference Group

With the exception of the three minor groups who had their origin in the Russian homeland, the majority of the immigrants to Kansas and the other western states, although coming from different congregations in the Molotschna with slightly different religious views, yet forgot these variations sufficiently here to unite in the promotion of certain early essential and common religious and educational enterprises—schools, missions, relief, and other charitable and common cultural interests. For the purpose largely of promoting their common school interests a number of them in 1877 organized the Kansas Conference. Later, with the affiliation of the Bavarian congregation at Halstead, Kansas, and the Prussian group at Beatrice, Nebraska, the name was changed to the Western District Conference. Those who located in Minnesota and Dakota formed the Northern District Conference. Nearly all of these congregations in course of time, beginning with Alexanderwohl in 1876, joined the General Conference Mennonite Church, and today form the largest contingent of that body. With the exception of their special school problems, described elsewhere, their religious history has been largely merged with that of the General Conference. Bethel College remains the special charge of the Western District Conference and a local school corporation. Among the other schools of the group are Freeman Junior College (South Dakota) and Canadian Mennonite Bible College (Manitoba).

The Mennonite Brethren

The next largest group was the Mennonite Brethren, which had its origin in Russia in the early sixties of the past century, and was imported into America with the immigrants of the seventies. The question of early origins need not detain us here except to mention only the bare facts of the beginnings of the church. The movement had its origin in the Gnadenfeld congregation in the Molotschna, a congregation in which there prevailed a much stronger interest in evangelism, prayer meetings, and mission festivals than was usually found in the churches at this time. A frequent visitor to these mission festivals was Pastor Wüst, a fiery preacher and evangelist from the nearby German Evangelical colony, a sort of John Wesley widely traveled throughout South Russia, whose active participation in these Mennonite meetings gave great impetus to the evangelistic movement already under way.

As a result of these influences a small group of laymen from Gnadenfeld and surrounding congregations, dissatisfied with what they regarded as the formalism of the churches in general, and desirous of a more definite recognition of sin consciousness and a freer expression of the religious experiences in worship than that which generally prevailed, withdrew from their congregations, formed a separate organization, selected a ministry, petitioned the czar's government for a special charter as an independent Mennonite body, and began the expansion of their new faith. Other groups followed, and so was started another branch of the Russian Mennonite church. A good summary of the beliefs of the group in the early stages is perhaps best told in the words of P. C. Hiebert:

1. A definite religious experience followed by a changed life, as a prerequisite of admission to membership.

2. Baptism by immersion upon confession of faith as the only recognized form.
3. A negative reaction against all tendencies toward formalism as it hindered early church procedure, and toward systematic religious instruction of children.
4. Definite opposition to all participation in military training and service.
5. Limiting communion to baptized members in good standing in the local church.
6. Active evangelism characterized by a keen personal interest in the personal conversion and salvation of one's associates.
7. A thorough study of all the Scriptures, which is recognized as the word of God, and an urgent demand that every member live up to what God requires in the Bible of those who have accepted Christ as their personal Saviour.

This new branch of the church had a slow growth at first. By the time of the American migration they numbered about six hundred. Small, scattered bands were found in almost all of the Mennonite groups that landed in America during the seventies; but there was no organized church life among them until 1879. The arrival, in 1885, of Abraham Schellenberg, their first organizer in America, initiated an aggressive campaign for church extension. By 1887 the membership was about twelve hundred, and has grown until today there are more than 27,000 members, about equally divided between the United States and Canada. A large percentage of the Canadian section consists of recent immigrants. There are in addition about 2,000 Mennonite Brethren scattered through the Mennonite colonies in Paraguay, Uruguay, and Brazil.

The Mennonite Brethren stress especially the need of a definite experience in conversion, and are still strongly evangelistic in their religious worship and activities. The mission interest has always been live among them, and they have numerous stations both at home and abroad. Being immersionists, they are quite friendly toward the Baptists and occasionally have lost some members to them. At first they also affiliated in educational work with McPherson College, in Kansas, a Church of the Brethren institution, but since 1908 have a college of their own, Tabor College at Hillsboro, Kansas, which became a conference school in 1934. Later schools were added in Fresno and Winnipeg. They have also co-operated freely, and taken a prominent part, with other Mennonite branches in recent years, in the foreign relief work and common opposition to military service.

The Krimmer Mennonite Brethren

Jacob A. Wiebe, the elder in a Kleine Gemeinde congregation in Crimea, coming under the influence of an evangelistic revival movement several years before the American migration, withdrew with his congregation from the somewhat formal church of his early youth. He introduced several innovations into his worship in keeping with his new-found experience and formed a new organization. In 1874 this congregation, following the general trek to the United States, founded on the virgin plains of Kansas, near the present town of Hillsboro, the only Russian-type farm village of the entire migration within the state, naming it Gnadenau.

These "Krimmer Brethren" were quite similar to the Mennonite Brethren, both in their religious spirit and in their forms of worship, except that the former immersed their converts forward, the latter backward. They were fervidly evangelistic in their religious activities, and perhaps well in advance of their other Russian brethren in forbidding the sale of tobacco and liquor in their early village, Gnadenau. They did not favor affiliation with the recreational and political life of the outside world, but they did strongly favor Sunday schools, evangelistic services, and missionary work. In 1961 the Krimmer Mennonite Brethren merged with the Mennonite Brethren to form one official body. At the time of merger they numbered about 1,750 members.

The Kleine Gemeinde

The Kleine Gemeinde (now officially known as the Evangelical Mennonite Church) owes its beginning to one Claas Reimer of the Molotschna colony, a sensitive soul of a very conservative character, who early in the past century found fault with his church for laxness in the application of disciplinary measures against erring members, and also for excessive strictness, on the other hand, on the part of the civil officials in the Mennonite villages in the administering of local police power over recalcitrant fellow Mennonites. This controversy finally led to the withdrawal of a small group from the main body in 1820, which, because it remained small in Russia, became known as the Kleine Gemeinde. The Reimer following migrated to America in the middle seventies, a small group locating in Manitoba, and another in Jefferson County, Nebraska. The latter, however, later moved almost en masse to southwestern Kansas. This small branch of the church remains conservative in its practices, and opposed to worldly conformity. In recent years they have accepted Sunday schools, young people's meetings, and singing classes. During the eighties and nineties many of them went over to the Church of God in Christ, Mennonite. In 1963 the membership of the Evangelical Mennonite Conference was about 2,800 in the United States, Canada, and Mexico. There are additional Kleine Gemeinde churches in Mexico and British Honduras that do not belong to this conference, with a combined membership of 250.

The Evangelical Mennonite Brethren

This group traces its inception to two pioneer ministers among the Russian immigrants—Isaac Peters of Nebraska, and Aaron Wall of Minnesota. Peters was an active promoter of the emigration movement in Russia in 1874, and for that reason was ordered into exile by his government. Later he reached America and became a member of the Bethesda Church at Henderson, Nebraska. Because of his conservative leanings and demand for rigid restrictions against participation in certain prevailing customs of his day, including among others the use of tobacco and following the popular styles of dress, he withdrew from his congregation and organized a separate body known for some years as the "Peters Church."

At the same time an incident along somewhat similar lines took place in the Mountain Lake settlement in Minnesota, under the leadership of Aaron Wall. The Wall followers for a number of years were called the "Bruderthal Congregation." These Wall and Peters groups, together with several other small independent congregations of like mind, organized themselves finally into a conference which they called the "Defenseless Mennonites of North America," later, in 1937, changed to the "Evangelical Mennonite Brethren." Many of the early distinctive demands of this church have since been modified, but they are still conservative in their practices. They are actively evangelistic, however, and support a strong mission and relief program. The present membership is about 3,000, which includes 200 in Paraguay. In 1953 they affiliated with the Evangelical Mennonite Church. (see p. 118). These two groups have merged their publishing interests and have organized a Conference of Evangelical Mennonites, but each group has thus far retained its own individuality.

Canadian Mennonite Groups

Several Mennonite branches have congregations in both Canada and the United States. Several others are confined to Canada only. Among those who have members on both sides and have already been described are the Mennonite Brethren; the Krimmer Mennonite Brethren; the Kleine Gemeinde; the Church of God in Christ, Mennonite; the Evangelical Mennonite Brethren; and the General Conference Mennonite Church. The largest number of the western Canadian Mennonites belong to either the Mennonite Brethren or the Conference of Mennonites in Canada, affiliated respectively with either the Mennonite Brethren Church of North America or the General Conference Mennonite Church.

It must be stated, however, that not all congregations belonging to the Conference of Mennonites in Canada are automatically members of the General Conference Mennonite Church. Each local congregation applies for membership. Not all congregations have yet joined the General Conference Mennonite Church. The following is a brief description of the major groups of Manitoba, of which some are also found in Saskatchewan.

In 1937 the Rudnerweide Mennonite Church was organized by Wilhelm H. Falk through the separation of a group from the Sommerfeld Mennonite Church, which was more evangelistic and more progressive. The migration of the most conservative element from Manitoba to Mexico and Paraguay, after World War I, and the coming of Mennonite immigrants from Russia after World Wars I and II, greatly affected and changed the spiritual and cultural life of the Mennonites in Manitoba.

The Bergthal Mennonite Church, which originated under the leadership of Johann Funk in 1890, spearheaded educational progress and helped H. H. Ewert in the establishment of the Mennonite Collegiate Institute at Gretna and the organization of the Canadian Mennonite Conference in 1902, which most of the non-M.B. immigrants coming to Canada after World War I and World War II joined. Most of the congregations of this conference are members of the General Conference Mennonite Church, but the large Bergthal Church, with over 4,000 baptized members, has thus far remained outside the General Conference.

Manitoba Mennonite Conferences and Churches

Church	Year Founded	Location
Chortitza Mennonite Church	1874	East Reserve
Old Colony Mennonite Church (Reinland)	1875	West Reserve
Bergthal Mennonite Church	1880	West Reserve
Sommerfeld Mennonite Church	1890	West Reserve
Rudnerweide Mennonite Church	1937	West Reserve

The religious and cultural life of the Manitoba Mennonites was marked by very conservative attitudes. The immigrants coming from the Bergthal settlement in Russia settled under the leadership of Gerhard Wiebe on the East Reserve. This was the nucleus for the Bergthal Mennonite Church. The Old Colony or Chortitza and Fürstenland Mennonites settled on the West Reserve, establishing the Reinland Mennonite Church, better known since as the Old Colony Mennonites under the leadership of Elder Johann Wiebe from Fürstenland.

In 1880 Elder Johann Wiebe through a brotherhood meeting reorganized the Reinland Mennonite Church of the West Reserve, making adherence to the old principles and practices a test of church membership. Many of the Old Colony Mennonites at this time joined the Bergthal group of the West Reserve, which had moved in from the East Reserve and had organized under the leadership of Elder Gerhard Wiebe of the East Reserve an independent church with Johann Funk as elder. However, Johann Funk was too progressive for some of the Bergthal Mennonites of the West Reserve. In 1890 most of the group rejected his leadership and organized what became known as the Sommerfeld Church, since its elder, Abraham Dörksen, lived in the village of Sommerfeld. Elder Johann Funk and his following continued under the name Bergthal Mennonite Church. In the East Reserve the Bergthal Church became known as the Chortitza Mennonite Church, since its elder resided in the village of Chortitza. Thus by the turn of the century the descendants of the original Chortitza settlement in Russia had divided into the large Old Colony Mennonite Church of the West Reserve, with a less conservative Sommerfeld Church and a rather progressive Bergthal Mennonite Church nearby, and a Chortitza Mennonite Church of the East Reserve which was spiritually and culturally most closely related to the Sommerfeld group.

CHAPTER 22

The General Conference
Mennonite Church

The General Conference Mennonite Church is the second largest of the different branches of the Mennonite denomination, and had its source during the middle of the past century as a unification movement in three widely scattered centers—Pennsylvania, Ontario, and Iowa. Chief among its promoters was John H. Oberholtzer, one of the leaders in the formation of the Eastern Pennsylvania District Conference in 1847, as already described. Even after his withdrawal from the Franconia Conference, Oberholtzer was hopeful of a reconciliation with his former brethren, as well as of a further union of a larger circle of Mennonite congregations. This cause he ardently espoused in his church paper, the *Christliches Volksblatt,* the former *Religiöser Botschafter,* as well as in a pamphlet, *Verantwortung und Erläuterung,* written in 1860.

The other two centers of the unification movement were in Ontario, where Daniel Hoch was the leader of a small group after 1853, and Lee County, Iowa, where Daniel Krehbiel and Christian Schowalter from the West Point and Zion congregations were outstanding. These two congregations held a joint meeting at the West Point church in 1859 for the purpose, according to a resolution passed at the meeting, to "devise ways on the one hand for the centralization of the Mennonite churches, but chiefly on the other for supplying isolated families with the Gospel blessings."

Encouraged by the success of this initial effort, the leaders of the movement issued an invitation to such other Mennonite congregations as might be interested to meet again the next year at the same place to discuss the further possibilities of united effort.

This conference, if such it can be called, met in due time at West Point, Iowa, on May 28, 1860, and was composed of delegates from the two above-mentioned Iowa churches, a minister from a neighboring congregation, and Oberholtzer and another delegate representing the Pennsylvania churches. Although unpretentious and local in character, the assembly drew up a set of resolutions which it hoped would serve as a common platform upon which all Mennonites might unite for the extension of the mission and other vital interests of the church. Following are the resolutions:

1. That all branches of the Mennonite denomination in North America, regardless of minor differences, should extend to each other the hand of fellowship.

2. That fraternal relations shall be severed only when a person or church abandons the fundamental doctrines of the denomination; namely, those concerning baptism, the oath, etc., as indeed all the principles which we with Menno base solely upon the Gospel as received from Jesus Christ and His apostles.

3. That no brother shall be found guilty of heresy unless his error can be established on unequivocal Scripture evidence.

4. That the General Conference shall consider no excommunication as Scripturally valid unless a real transgression or neglect conflicting with the demands of Scripture exists.

5. That every church or district shall be entitled to continue, without molestation or hindrance and amenable only to their own conscience, any rules or regulations they may have adopted for their own government, provided they do not conflict with the tenets of our general confession.

6. That if a member of a church, because of existing customs or ordinances of his church, shall desire to sever his connection and unite with some other church of the General Conference, such action shall not be interfered with.

Thus was launched what it was decided to call the General Conference of the Mennonite Church of North America. At the meeting the following year at Wadsworth, Ohio, a new article, discouraging membership in secret societies, was added to the platform of the year before; and the first steps were taken to collect funds for the establishing of a theological school.

From this time on the conference movement had a steady growth. Each succeeding meeting showed a steady gain in the number of affiliating congregations. At first the additions came largely from the Oberholtzer Pennsylvania churches. But in 1875 the Swiss congregation at Berne, Indiana, represented by S. F. Sprunger, was present. The following year at a special session, the first of the Russian contingent, Alexanderwohl, represented by Heinrich Richert, was admitted. After this, most of the growth came from the Russian churches in the west, whose sympathies had been won by the General

Conference both because of the help the latter had given them during the early years of settlement on the western prairies, and also because of a common interest in missions, not yet aroused by other native branches of the denomination. The meeting in 1893 was held at Bluffton, Ohio, when for the first time the Swiss churches at Bluffton and Dalton, Ohio, and the former Amish congregations at Trenton, Ohio, and Noble, Iowa, joined the movement. Since then numerous independent congregations, having no other conference connections for some reason or other, have been added. Many of the recent immigrant Russian congregations, both in Canada and in the United States, have increased the numerical strength of the General Conference. In 1962 the entire baptized membership of the Conference totaled about 55,000, of whom nearly 36,000 were in the United States, more than 16,000 in Canada (this does not include some groups in Canada [Bergthal, etc.] and the mission churches), and 2,500 in South America.

The two questions that occupied much of the attention of the conference sessions during the first twenty years were education and missions. As early as 1862 the movement for establishing a school for training church workers and providing a Christian education in general was initiated. But the institution, which was to be located at Wadsworth, and was known as the "Christian Education Institution of the Mennonite Denomination," did not open its doors until 1868, with Christian Schowalter as principal, to be succeeded several years later by C. J. van der Smissen, an imported minister from Germany. The instruction was in the German language, and the curriculum was designed largely to train young men for the church; young women were never admitted. The school continued only ten years, closing in 1878 largely because of financial difficulties, and also lack of agreement among its supporters over educational policies. Many of the early ministers and missionaries of the church, however, got their first inspiration for their work from this pioneer educational institution.

The other objective of the Conference was missions, an objective still very much in the fore in all its sessions. The General Conference was the first branch of the church to inaugurate missionary activities among the American Indians, a work still carried on effectively in three states. In 1900 the first foreign station was established in India. Since then mission work was extended into China, and later transferred to Japan. This branch of the church today supports about one hundred missionaries at home and abroad.

131

It will thus be observed that the General Conference Mennonite Church was not originally meant to be a separate branch of the church, but rather a union of the various groups for the effective promotion of common church interests still in an embryo stage among the different branches at that time—missions, education, publication, and in later years relief work. To make the attainment of this goal possible, the slight differences which separated the different groups had to be minimized, and only the fundamentals of Mennonitism, upon which all could agree, emphasized. The sessions of the Conference, therefore, have remained almost entirely advisory, with matters of discipline and much of local church practices left to local regional conferences and congregations. And yet though it aims to be merely an advisory body, the fact that it must set up definite qualifications for membership in the body gives it somewhat the character of a separate ecclesiastical body; and so it is usually regarded.

The conference meets every three years, and is composed of delegates elected by the participating congregations, which are given voting power according to the size of their individual membership. These sessions are devoted largely to the discussion of reports from the various standing boards—Missions, Education, Publication, and in recent years, Peace and Emergency Relief, and such committees as have been appointed for special purposes. Church government among the congregations is strictly congregational, each minister usually being an elder with full power to administer all the religious rites demanded of the church. There are no superior officers, and the title "bishop," common among the (old) Mennonites and the Amish, is unknown.

Since the close of the Wadsworth school in 1878, the General Conference has assumed no further obligation, as a conference project, for maintaining educational institutions, preferring to leave that responsibility to the district conferences and local organizations. Thus Bethel College is the joint responsibility of the Western District and a local school association; Freeman College is sponsored by the local Dakota churches; Bluffton College by the Eastern and Central district conferences. The Canadian Mennonite Bible College (Winnipeg) is a project of the churches in Canada. The numerous small vacation schools in which German and Bible played a leading role, once popular but now declining, were local congregational projects. But a number of local Bible schools, largely supported by private and local associations, are still in existence. A seminary known as Witmarsum Theological Seminary operated at Bluffton, Ohio, from 1918 to 1930. In 1945 the Mennonite Biblical Seminary was opened in Chicago and then in 1958 it was moved to Elkhart, Indiana, where it is affiliated with Goshen College Biblical Seminary in the Associated Mennonite Biblical Seminaries.

Since World War I the Conference has carried on, in co-operation with most of the other branches of the church, especially through the Mennonite Central Committee, an extensive relief program, especially in behalf of their brethren in Russia, but also in more recent years among the refugees and the suffering in the war-stricken areas. This branch of the church has been active also in the promotion of the peace cause. The Russian immigrants of 1874 were especially concerned about this question. For some years there has been an active peace committee. Since World War I this part of the church program has been given increased attention. Together with representatives of the (old) Mennonites, and the Mennonite Brethren, as well as the other groups, a joint work has been carried on which has done much to keep alive the peace cause among the Mennonites, and also witness to those outside the denomination.

The General Conference and Bethel College operate jointly the Mennonite Press and the Publication Board publishes the official organs of the church, *The Mennonite* and *Der Bote,* an annual *Year Book,* Sunday-school supplies, and numerous other books and pamphlets of a religious and denominational character.

CHAPTER 23

Some Related Groups

The Hutterian Brethren

The Hutterian Brethren received their name from Jacob Hutter, leader of the Anabaptists in Moravia in the early sixteenth century, who suffered martyrdom at the stake for his religious faith in 1536. The Hutterites differed from the other Anabaptists of their day, and the later Mennonites, in living in a collective community, "sharing their material as well as their spiritual gifts" on Scriptural, not economic grounds. It was this religious sanction of their communistic system, no doubt the most potent of all sanctions, that gave their society the sustaining and perpetuating force that has kept it alive all through the centuries, down to the present day. The Hutterites are, perhaps, the oldest of all these communistic societies still in existence. All others which were based on mere economic or humanitarian grounds long since have run their course.

The Hutterian Brethren lived in small groups of from fifteen to twenty-five families in communities called Bruderhofs, which became almost complete, self-sufficient economic and social units. After several centuries of oppression and persecution, often almost complete annihilation, and a series of treks from Moravia through Hungary and modern Rumania in search of freedom of conscience, without losing either their religion or their determination to share all their goods in common, they finally arrived in Russia during the latter part of the eighteenth century, to join the Mennonites one hundred years later in their trek from Russia to America.

In America the first group of two hundred and fifty souls located a Bruderhof in 1874 along the Missouri River near Yankton, South Dakota, on a tract of land of twenty-five hundred acres for which they paid twenty-five thousand dollars, seventeen thousand of which was cash. A little later two other Bruderhofs were located on the James River. From these three original colonies other daughter colonies later developed up the James River, until by 1918 there were some twenty in all with a total population of nearly three thousand. The social and economic life in these Bruderhofs repeated that of the European models. Families lived in compartments under the same roof. All ate at a common table. All the fruits of their common labor went into a common fund, managed by a superintendent (*Wirt*). There was no private property except the clothes they wore. No one had any private spending money. Most of the colonies were located near the river, and in the early days at least milling became a favorite side issue. Fishing and sheep raising were also emphasized. Life in the Bruderhof was simple, primitive, and largely carefree for the individual. There was never any anxiety about poverty, or old-age troubles, or unemployment. Clothes were largely homemade. As late as the beginning of World War I, the hum of the spinning wheel was still a familiar sound in the women's quarters of the big houses.

Social contacts with the outside world, too, for the average individual were not frequent. There was a school in each Bruderhof, with a self-made teacher who had little if any outside training. Lack of transportation facilities, and lack of spending money, made visits even to the nearby villages unattractive and useless. The only social contacts with the outside world were occasional visits to the other Bruderhofs.

Materially, this kind of community life was a great success. Profits were large; expenses were low; and there was little waste on luxuries. All the surplus profits were invested in more land areas for taking care of the increasing population in future additional Bruderhofs.

Doctrinally, the Hutterites, who confined their religious worship and religious terminology to the German language, and for that reason called themselves *Hutterische Brüder,* retained almost to the letter the ancient faith of the fathers, including a strict interpretation of the doctrine of nonresistance. The Hutterian Brethren of the Dakotas were perhaps the only group among the peace churches in World War I whose young men, almost without exception, refused public service of any sort if connected with the war department. Two of these young men, because of persistent refusal to compromise their convictions regarding military service, were so abused and mistreated in the military camps, and later in the prisons at Alcatraz and in Leavenworth, that they died of injuries received there. The home churches, too, refused to contribute to the various war drives unless assured that

135

their contributions would not be used for direct war purposes. Under pressure, however, and with a halfway promise that their money would be applied to some public efforts not directly connected with the war machine, they contributed some thirty thousand dollars. The local Councils of Defense, however, considering this amount insufficient, appeared at their Bruderhofs in force, and confiscated sufficent cattle and sheep to make up the amount they had allocated to them.

The State Council of Defense, too, desirous seemingly of either breaking up the Bruderhofs as independent units, or driving the Brethren out of the state entirely, brought suit against the colonies with the purpose of annulling the charters which had been granted some time earlier to the various Bruderhofs as religious organizations. In this the Council of Defense succeeded. The local courts annulled the charters, ordered the sale of all their property, and the distribution of all the proceeds to the individual members. This order made it impossible for the Hutterian Brethren to live a community life, and their religion made it impossible for them to do otherwise. Consequently, although the decision was appealed to higher courts, nearly all of the Bruderhofs sold their property at a great sacrifice, and made another trek to the prairie lands of Alberta and Manitoba, Canada, where they finally established a new series of Bruderhofs. Today the Hutterians number 10,000 members in Canada and nearly 4,000 in the United States.

The Brethren in Christ

[Note: This account of the history and faith of the Brethren in Christ is taken from a brief sketch prepared by Dr. A. W. Climenhaga.]

There are various opinions concerning the starting of the Brethren in Christ Church. The weight of evidence reveals that the work was not a split from another organized body of believers. The church was born in the cradle of the faiths of the Church of the Brethren, Mennonites, and Quakers. A group of twelve men who had experienced the knowledge of sins forgiven found themselves fellowshiping together for mutual benefit; and in order to keep the ordinances of baptism and the Lord's Supper, they considered joining one of the above-mentioned groups, but finally decided that they themselves

136

would organize by putting in leaders. They baptized one another and set apart several as ministers. This new organization stood for the principle of parity of all the members with Christ as their head. Some of the first ministers were Jacob Engle, Hans Engle, and Hans Winger. Jacob Engle was looked to more or less as the leader and thus became the overseer.

This organization took place about 1778 in Lancaster County, Pennsylvania, a short distance from the Susquehanna River. From this nearness to the river they were distinguished from other Brethren in the county as the River Brethren. For many years the church went by this name, "River Brethren," given them by other people. The same church was called Tunkers in a wing which developed in Canada. In 1862 it was finally decided to name the church, "The Brethren in Christ," but the organization was not chartered until 1904, when this became the legal name.

From 1779 to 1904 the church had a gradual growth. The first development was away from the river toward the city of Lancaster and the town of Manheim. Members were soon found in valleys of Cumberland and Lebanon counties as well as in Lancaster County. Three Districts were formed in Lancaster County with an Overseer over each. The Overseers of Districts finally were called Bishops and those who assisted them in preaching were called Elders. For many years no church buildings were built, but all the services were held in barns and houses. The first church building was erected in 1867 at Woodbury, Pennsylvania, not far from Altoona. Other sections of the state where members are found are Lykens Valley, Mifflin, Clinton, Center, and Lycoming counties, and Philadelphia and vicinity.

As early as 1789 some members moved to Canada. Hans Winger of Pennsylvania was the first Overseer there. It is claimed that Hans Winger was the first minister in Ontario outside of the English clergy to receive the privilege of performing marriages. Districts developed in Canada near Buffalo, New York, near Toronto, and one as far west as Saskatchewan, a total of six in all. After the church was established in Pennsylvania and Canada, a growth developed westward which reached as far west as California. The first state to receive members of this faith outside of Pennsylvania was Ohio. Soon after this some members moved from Ontario to the state of Indiana. Districts are also found in Michigan, Illinois, Kansas, Oklahoma, and Iowa. The states with the most members outside of Pennsylvania are

Ohio and Kansas. The total membership in 1959 was a little less than 7,000, grouped in 150 congregations.

On two different occasions divisions took place which divided the church into three parts. The first division was in 1843, when a number of members felt the church was departing from some of the original customs; so these separated and held separate services. This first group which separated had a very slow growth, and to this day they continue to hold their services in their houses and barns. They became known as Yorkers or Yorker Brethren, because some of the first members lived in York County, Pennsylvania. Most of the Yorker Brethren now live in Lancaster and Franklin counties.

The second division arose in 1852 when trouble resulted over the building of a place of worship. Mathias Brinser, a minister in the then called River Brethren Church near Middletown, Pennsylvania, decided there ought to be a place of worship where the members in his locality could meet regularly instead of using the barns and houses. Although requested by the Lancaster County Brethren not to build, he and his followers decided to continue nevertheless, and were consequently expelled by the main body in 1855. This new body of believers took for their name "United Zion's Children." Although still an independent group, they co-operate with the Brethren in Christ in a number of areas. In 1959 they had about 900 members.

As early as 1850 the Brethren in Christ became interested in mission work. The first form of this activity consisted in leaders traveling many miles by horseback to preach. It was not until 1871 that General Conference decided to give offerings throughout the church for a missionary fund and to appoint a mission board. At present there are two general mission boards—one for foreign work and one for home work, as well as a number of smaller boards. Home mission stations were started as early as 1889, but foreign work did not start till 1897, with the first station in Africa. The India Mission was started in 1905. Much of the awakening in relation to missions came through evangelistic efforts. The offerings for foreign work gradually increased from five hundred dollars in 1896 to over five thousand in 1910, twenty thousand in 1918, and over twenty-five thousand in 1931.

There was also a marked growth in home mission work. In 1918 there were city missions in Buffalo, New York; Chicago, Illinois; Des Moines, Iowa; Dayton, Ohio; and San Francisco, California. In 1919 stations were accepted by the church in Philadelphia and Chambersburg, Pennsylvania; Detroit, Michigan; and Welland, Ontario. Many rural stations have been opened in Pennsylvania, Virginia, Florida, Kentucky, and Ontario, as well as in some other states.

The church did not sponsor Sunday schools until one hundred years after it started. A few schools started a little earlier, but in some districts Sunday schools did not start until after 1900. General Conference called it a new movement in 1885.

In 1880 a church paper was established, named the *Evangelical Visitor*. A church publishing house was decided upon in 1917, now located at Nappanee, Indiana.

The church supports four institutions of learning—two colleges and two secondary schools. The question of starting a church school came to General Conference in 1897, but the work was not started until 1909.

Messiah Bible College started as a Bible School and Missionary Training Home in 1909 in Harrisburg, Pennsylvania. In 1911 the school was moved to Grantham, Pennsylvania, ten miles from Harrisburg. The institution was rechartered in 1924 as Messiah Bible College. Upland College, located at Upland, California, was started in 1920. Jabbok Bible School and Academy opened in 1925 at Thomas, Oklahoma. The Ontario Bible School and Academy started in 1932 and is located near Fort Erie, Ontario, on the bank of the Niagara River.

Benevolent institutions have been well supported for the care of children and the aged folks. The church supports an orphanage near Morrison, Illinois, called Mount Carmel Orphanage, and one at Florin, Pennsylvania, called Messiah Orphanage. The Messiah Rescue and Benevolent Home for old people is located in Harrisburg, Pennsylvania.

The church teaches justification by faith, holiness and empowerment, divine healing, trine immersion, washing the saints' feet, holy kiss, nonresistance, Scriptural veiling, and the general resurrection of the dead. Only such as profess a knowledge of saving grace are baptized and taken into the church as communicant members. The women members wear the prayer veiling and are known as sisters. The men are known as brethren and are expected with the sisters not to conform to worldly practices and customs in business or pleasure which are not considered in keeping with the teachings of Jesus. Love feasts and communion services are held in each church at least once a year.

139

The church is controlled by a general conference held annually in various parts of the brotherhood. The officers of the church are bishops, ministers, and deacons. A large amount of the work of the church centers in boards. The church institutions are controlled by boards of trustees, which boards are subject to General Conference.

During the past twenty-five years the Brethren in Christ have drawn increasingly closer to the Mennonite circle until today they are regarded as wholly within the family. E. J. Swalm is a member of the Presidium of the Mennonite World Conference, while C. N. Hostetter, Jr., long-time president of Messiah College, is chairman of the Mennonite Central Committee and occasionally teaches in special sessions of the Associated Mennonite Biblical Seminaries. Messiah and Upland Colleges are also members of the Council of Mennonite and Affiliated Colleges.

CHAPTER 24

Keeping the Faith

The American Mennonites, it will be observed, are not a homogeneous and united people, with a single ecclesiastical organization. But, owing to a number of causes—different European origins, widely scattered settlements in America, difference of opinion on questions of social practice and custom, and a loosely organized congregational form of government—some twenty varieties of Mennonites have developed through the two hundred and eighty years since the coming of the first Mennonites to America in 1683. It must be remembered, however, that many of these groups are very small, and that only seven organized groups have more than 4,000 baptized members.

As repeatedly stated in this treatise, these differences are not always based on fundamental religious beliefs but often on less consequential though irreconcilable details of religious forms and social practices, sometimes largely survivals of earlier usages which were not originally adopted as matters of church regulation. Theologically all Mennonite groups have remained conservative and fairly well united. According to Harold S. Bender, in an address before the All-Mennonite Congress at Amsterdam in 1936, American Mennonites agree on these fundamentals:

1. The divine authority and adequacy of the Word of God.
2. The necessity of a holy life in obedience to that Word of God.
3. The high calling and place of the church as distinct from the state.
4. Separation between the church and the world.
5. The abandonment of all carnal warfare and force, and the actual practice of the Gospel of peace.

The essential doctrinal unity of the American Mennonites is best evidenced by their common acceptance of one or the other of the original confessions of faith. In 1963, however, the (old) Mennonite

Church, in its biennial session of Mennonite General Conference, adopted a new Confession of Faith. Many still accept as a satisfactory statement of their religious beliefs, with a few modifications, the old Dortrecht Confession of 1632, which, in addition to the commonly accepted Mennonite doctrines, includes the practice of avoidance, or shunning, a practice abandoned, however, by all except a few. Foot washing also is prescribed, which is still commonly observed by most, but not all of the groups.

The General Conference has favored the broader Cornelis Ris Confession of 1747, which agrees with that of Dortrecht on the fundamentals, but varies somewhat in certain details. It is slightly more philosophical than the latter, is silent on foot washing, and does not mention the practice of avoidance. Marriage with "unbelievers" is forbidden by it, and divorce also, except on Scriptural grounds.

On the doctrine of nonresistance and opposition to war, the American Mennonites have kept the faith. Up to 1917 American wars were fought largely by volunteers. Since there was no conscription except in the Civil War the war problem was not a serious matter for those religiously opposed to participation in war. In the Colonial period, both Pennsylvania and Virginia, where Mennonites were settled before the Revolutionary War, as well as the federal government since that war, generally manifested the greatest consideration for the religious scruples of those conscientiously opposed to war—the Mennonites, Quakers, and Dunkers. Exemption from actual service was always provided. During the Civil War, in the conscription act passed near the close, provision was made for draftees to furnish substitutes; but for those conscientiously opposed, exemption was made possible by an outright money payment of three hundred dollars. The Confederacy passed a similar law, but with a five hundred dollar payment. Due to the great need of men, however, in the South near the close of the war, all exemptions were repealed, and most of the drafted young Mennonite men in Virginia escaped to the western part of the state, or over the line into Pennsylvania.

It was not until the World War in 1917 that the faith of the Mennonites was tried to the limit in America. The universal conscription act of that year required the complete mobilization of the entire man power of the country, with no provision for substitutes or money payments. However, exemption from combatant service for those religiously opposed to war was provided for by the substitution of such service in the army as the President might declare to be non-combatant. The President, and not the one objecting, was to judge what service the latter could conscientiously assume. Some of the young Mennonites accepted this service. But many others refused to compromise their convictions by accepting an alternate service which they held to be as definitely connected with the war system as unconditional participation in combatant service. To these men, if carrying a gun was inconsistent with their beliefs, so was driving a munitions truck, or sitting at a war office desk writing out pay checks, or even serving in a military hospital. The term "conscientious objector" first became known during this war. These men who refused all service were court-martialed; some were furloughed to do farm work; a few were sent to France for reconstruction work; about two hundred were sent to prison at Fort Leavenworth, sentenced to serve from ten to twenty years, but all were released soon after the war was over.

The Canadian government, likewise, was most liberal in its attitude toward those conscientiously opposed to military service, special provision being made in all their military acts for Mennonites, Dunkers, and Quakers. Exemption provisions were enacted into all the militia acts of Ontario in the early part of the century; and into the Dominion Act of 1868. When the Russian Mennonites made an appeal for complete exemption in 1874, at the time of their immigration to Manitoba, an Order in Council granted the request, a promise scrupulously kept by the Canadian government during World War I. The Canadian conscription act of World War II was not quite so liberal in its treatment of the Mennonites and other conscientious objectors, but provision was still made for complete exemption from military service.

Our own conscription act of 1917 had taken the Mennonites by surprise. They had always taken military exemption in America for granted, and were not prepared to meet the demands made upon them by this unexpected act. But profiting by their experience during the World War, many Mennonites in the years that followed were constrained to reappraise their peace principles in the light of the new demands that might be made of them in possible future conflicts; to clarify their own thought in advance, and fortify their resolution to remain firm in the faith if the worst should happen; and especially acquaint the general public, as well as the governing authorities, with their peace principles and ideals. Some of the larger branches of the church appointed peace committees (the oldest one being that of the [old] Mennonites, set up in 1925), which did most excellent work in the promotion of all the above objectives.

With the exception of a few Dutch immigrants to Germantown in 1683 and the years immediately following till 1707, and another Dutch group that came to Elkhart County, Indiana, in 1852, the American Mennonites are of German origin, at least linguistically and culturally, even though not always of original German racial stock. The Palatine immigrants to Pennsylvania in the early eighteenth century, as well as their Swiss brethren, who came to the Middle West one hundred years later, were of original Swiss stock, though from the German section of Switzerland. The Alsatian Amish, who came about the same time, were also originally of the same Swiss stock. The Russians, who came in 1874, were of original Dutch stock who had for two hundred years in Eastern Prussia developed among themselves a German culture, which another hundred years in Russia could not destroy. And so all Mennonites formerly read German books and spoke some sort of German language. They used high German in the pulpit, if possible, and some sort of German dialect in their everyday conversation—Pennsylvania Dutch, Alsatian patois, Bavarian dialect, *Platt* and *Schweizer Dietsch*. German remained the official language of the churches until well toward the end of the nineteenth century, even among the Pennsylvania Mennonites. It is just now passing out among the Russian immigrants of 1874, but still remains well entrenched among the Old Order Amish, the Old Colonists of Mexico, and the Sommerfelder of Canada; and of course among all the recent Russian immigrants in South America and Canada.

Until after World War I the American Mennonites were almost exclusively a farming people. They were farmers in Europe and they remained farmers here. They have a reputation as being among America's best farmers; and they are found in some of the most productive areas in the country. This becomes evident by the mere mention of some of the regions in which they are found in large numbers—Lancaster County, Pennsylvania; Wayne County, Ohio; McLean County, Illinois, which with Lancaster County several years ago was proclaimed one of the two richest agricultural counties in the entire country by the United States Department of Agriculture; Johnson County, Iowa; Harvey County, Kansas; and the Western

Reserve in Manitoba. Mennonites have seldom if ever been found on poor soil. During the land boom of World War I the highest price ever paid for ordinary farm land in American history was paid for a corn farm of 160 acres in the Mennonite community near Flanagan, Illinois—seven hundred dollars per acre.

Mennonite churches, consequently, were country churches, always well attended and well supported. A few congregations were found in the smaller cities, or in smaller towns in the midst of large Mennonite rural communities; but, with one or two exceptions, there were no indigenous churches in the large metropolitan cities. The period since World War II has been one of rapid urbanization, however, bringing important changes in the life of the Mennonite churches which promise to be increasingly significant for the coming generation.

With the exception of a few attempts by the more progressive wings of the church, the Mennonites did not enter very extensively into mission work before 1900. Sunday schools, in the main, started almost simultaneously in the larger and more progressive branches soon after the Civil War; home missions in the eighties; and foreign missions not until the nineties. Today all but a few of the conservative branches carry on an extensive mission enterprise, both home and foreign. With the exception of the Mennonite Brethren in Christ and some sections of the (old) Mennonites, particularly Lancaster, Mennonites, in the main, have not been especially successful in their home mission efforts. City missions have not been a fruitful source of large additions to the church. Consequently, today, in the main, with the exceptions just mentioned, the American Mennonites are the children and children's children of European ancestors, with few additions from American stock. Mennonite family names are predominantly duplicates of those in Europe. The growth of Mennonitism in America has been rather the swarming of a people than the expansion of a faith.

Interest in higher education, too, grew apace with that of other progressive activities. Wadsworth was founded in 1868; Halstead, in 1883; Gretna, in 1891; Bethel, 1893; Goshen, 1894; Bluffton, 1900; Rosthern, 1902; Freeman, 1903; Tabor, 1908; Hesston, 1909; Eastern Mennonite School, 1917; Lancaster Mennonite School, 1942. Others were added since World War II.

Beginning after World War I and continuing to the present, all branches of the church have been carrying on a most commendable

145

program of relief among the war sufferers in Europe. In this work all have shown the finest spirit of co-operation.

In church polity the American Mennonites were originally strictly congregational, each congregation being an independent ecclesiastical unit. Conferences were at first merely advisory bodies, but gradually some became authoritative. A few slight exceptions should be noted. The bishops in some conferences of (old) Mennonites have supervision over more than one congregation. Among the more conservative groups some ministers are still selected from the congregation by lot and serve without pay and with little or no special training. All the Progressives, however, demand an educated ministry; and the tendency is in that direction among the Moderates.

In conclusion, the writer of this brief summary of the history of the American Mennonites feels that he can find no more appropriate remarks with which to close this sketch than those uttered by Harold S. Bender, speaking for the American Mennonites, in the closing sentences of his address before the Amsterdam World Mennonite Congress of 1936:

"We are profoundly grateful that our heavenly Father's providence through the course of the history of the past two centuries has placed us in such a goodly land with free and progressive institutions, where we have had an almost unparalleled opportunity with perfect freedom of conscience, unhampered by the attitude and activities of a state church, to unfold the content of our Mennonite heritage, and to develop whatever genius there may be in our Mennonite people. As we look back over four hundred years of history we are convinced that God has preserved our Mennonite brotherhood for a purpose, and as I know American Mennonites, I am convinced that they are in general possessed of a deep desire to fulfill this purpose, to know the will of God, and to do it in full obedience to His Word. We have a spiritual heritage that is needed in this modern age. Only if we are true to this heritage and to God's call have we a right to a continued existence. God grant that we may be true."

Statistical Section
TABLE 1
Mennonite World Membership

AFRICA — 66,231

Zaire (Congo), 44,205; Tanzania, 7,063; Ethiopia, 600; Rhodesia, 8,500; Zambia, 1,500; Nigeria, 3,962; Ghana, 301; others, 100.

ASIA — 58,472

Indonesia, 21,760; India 24,274; China, 4,000; Taiwan, 528; Japan, 1,518; Vietnam, 85.

EUROPE — 99,374

Netherlands, 34,700; Russia, 45,000; Germany, 14,248; Switzerland, 3,000; France, 2,034; Italy, 60; Luxembourg, 160; Belgium, 50; Austria, 93; England, 29.

NORTH AMERICA — 251,636

United States, 183,773; Canada, 67,863.

LATIN AMERICA — 32,718

Panama, 292; Haiti, 23; Costa Rica, 38; Guatemala, 33; Guiana, 14; El Salvador, 19; Mexico, 11,906; Belize, 1,248; Honduras, 362; Dominican Republic, 571; Puerto Rico, 672; Jamaica, 299; Colombia, 920; Brazil, 2,767; Uruguay, 688; Argentina, 3,438; Paraguay, 8,477; Bolivia, 951.

WORLD TOTAL — 508,431

— Mennonite Life (September 1972)

TABLE 2
BAPTIZED MEMBERS OF ALL MENNONITE BODIES IN UNITED STATES AND CANADA, 1973°

Mennonite Body	United States	Canada	Total
Beachy Amish Mennonite Church....	3,699	320	4,019
Brethren in Christ Church.....	9,550	1,466	11,016
Church of God in Christ, Mennonite..	6,749	2,228	8,977
Chortiz Mennonites°°	.	1,800	1,800
Evangelical Mennonite Brethren			
Conference°°	1,821	1,645	3,466
Evangelical Mennonite Church.....	3,131	.	3,131
Evangelical Mennonite Conference			
(Kleine Gemeinde).........	.	4,000	4,000
Evangelical Mennonite Mission			
Conference (Rudnerweider)° ...		1,850	1,850
General Conference Mennonite	36,129		
Church..............	6,640	20,601	56,730
Hutterian Brethren..........		14,700	21,340
Mennonite Brethren Churches,			
General Conference of	16,030		33,295
Mennonite Church........	90,967	17,265	100,161
Non-Conference Hutterian-Mennonite		9,194	
Colonies..............	845		1,170
Old Colony Mennonite Church		325	
in Canada..............	.	3,168	3,168
Old Order Amish Mennonite Church .	22,550	650	23,200
Old Order & Wisler Mennonite			
Churches.............	6,200	2,180	8,380
Reformed Mennonite Church.....	553	193	746
Reinland Mennonites°°	.	800	800
Sommerfelder Mennonites°°	.	4,000	4,000
TOTALS..............	204,864	86,385	291,249

°From 1974 *Mennonite Yearbook,* Mennonite Publishing House, Scottdale, Pa. 15683.
°°1972 Report

CPSIA information can be obtained
at www.ICGtesting.com
Printed in the USA
LVHW051711310121
677942LV00013B/1759